Angel
Visions

Also by Doreen Virtue, Ph.D.

Books
THE CRYSTAL CHILDREN
ARCHANGELS AND ASCENDED MASTERS
EARTH ANGELS
MESSAGES FROM YOUR ANGELS
ANGEL VISIONS II
EATING IN THE LIGHT (with Becky Prelitz, M.F.T., R.D.)
THE CARE AND FEEDING OF INDIGO CHILDREN
HEALING WITH THE FAIRIES
*DIVINE PRESCRIPTIONS
HEALING WITH THE ANGELS
"I'D CHANGE MY LIFE IF I HAD MORE TIME"
*DIVINE GUIDANCE
CHAKRA CLEARING
ANGEL THERAPY
THE LIGHTWORKER'S WAY
CONSTANT CRAVING A–Z
CONSTANT CRAVING
THE YO-YO DIET SYNDROME
LOSING YOUR POUNDS OF PAIN

Audio Programs
ANGELS AMONG US (with Michael Toms)
MESSAGES FROM YOUR ANGELS (abridged audio book)
PAST-LIFE REGRESSION WITH THE ANGELS
*DIVINE PRESCRIPTIONS
THE ROMANCE ANGELS
CONNECTING WITH YOUR ANGELS (2-tape set and 6-tape set)
MANIFESTING WITH THE ANGELS
KARMA RELEASING
HEALING YOUR APPETITE, HEALING YOUR LIFE
HEALING WITH THE ANGELS
*DIVINE GUIDANCE
CHAKRA CLEARING
LOSING YOUR POUNDS OF PAIN (abridged audio book)

Oracle Cards (44 divination cards and guidebook)
HEALING WITH THE ANGELS ORACLE CARDS
HEALING WITH THE FAIRIES ORACLE CARDS
MESSAGES FROM YOUR ANGELS ORACLE CARDS
(card pack and booklet)
MAGICAL MERMAIDS AND DOLPHINS ORACLE CARDS

All of the above titles are available through your local bookstore.
All items except those with an asterisk (*) are available by calling
Hay House at (800) 654-5126.

Please visit the Hay House Website at: hayhouse.com and
Dr. Virtue's Website at AngelTherapy.com

Angel
Visions

True Stories of People Who Have Seen Angels,
and How *You* Can See Angels, Too!

Doreen Virtue, Ph.D.

HAY HOUSE, INC.
Carlsbad, California
London • Sydney • Johannesburg
Vancouver • Hong Kong

Published and distributed in the United States by: Hay House, Inc., P.O. Box 5100, Carlsbad, CA 92018-5100 • *Phone:* (760) 431-7695 or (800) 654-5126 • *Fax:* (760) 431-6948 or (800) 650-5115 • www.hayhouse.com • *Published and distributed in Australia by:* Hay House Australia Pty. Ltd., 18/36 Ralph St., Alexandria NSW 2015 • *Phone:* 612-9669-4299 • *Fax:* 612-9669-4144 • www.hayhouse.com.au • *Published and distributed in the United Kingdom by:* Hay House UK, Ltd. • Unit 62, Canalot Studios • 222 Kensal Rd., London W10 5BN • *Phone:* 44-20-8962-1230 • *Fax:* 44-20-8962-1239 • www.hayhouse.co.uk • *Published and distributed in the Republic of South Africa by:* Hay House SA (Pty), Ltd., P.O. Box 990, Witkoppen 2068 • *Phone/Fax:* 2711-7012233 • orders@psdprom.co.za • *Distributed in Canada by:* Raincoast • 9050 Shaughnessy St., Vancouver, B.C. V6P 6E5 • *Phone:* (604) 323-7100 • *Fax:* (604) 323-2600

Editorial: Jill Kramer • *Design:* Summer McStravick
Cover illustration: Corey Wolfe

The intent of the author is only to offer information of a general nature to help you in your quest for emotional and spiritual well-being. In the event you use any of the information in this book for yourself, which is your constitutional right, the author and the publisher assume no responsibility for your actions.

"A Mother's Eternal Love," excerpted from *Chocolate for a Woman's Soul,* by Kay Allenbaugh (Fireside/Simon & Schuster, 1997). Reprinted with permission.

Library of Congress Cataloging-in-Publication Data

Angel visions: true stories of people who have seen angels, and how you can see angels, too / [compiled by] Doreen Virtue.
     p. cm.
Includes bibliographical references.
ISBN 1-56170-712-0 (tradepaper)
1. Angels--Miscellanea. I. Virtue, Doreen.

BL477 .A54 2000
291.2'15--dc21

00-039583

ISBN 1-56170-712-0

07 06 05 04   14 13 12 11
1st printing, August 2000
11th printing, June 2004

Printed in Canada

꧁꧂꧁꧂꧁꧂

To Pop-Pop Ben, Grandma Pearl,
and Grandpa Fount Leroy Merrill,
Who Were Angels in My Visions

꧁꧂꧁꧂꧁꧂

Contents

PREFACE

Angel Visions

Have you ever seen an angel? Many people have. Perhaps you, too, have seen an angel and didn't know it. In this book, you'll meet people from all walks of life who have one thing in common: *They have had an angel vision.*

An angel vision is an experience of seeing the Divine, or that which is usually considered invisible. There is a diverse array of angel visions. Some people actually see Renaissance-type angels, complete with wings, with their eyes open. Other people experience their angels as an interaction with an apparition of a deceased loved one. For others, the angel vision comes during a dream, yet the dream is profound, extra-vivid, and often prophetic. Still others have interactions with Jesus, Mary, a saint, or an avatar.

Angel visions also involve pivotal meetings with helpful strangers, who either intervene or deliver an important message . . . and then vanish without a trace. And some people's angel visions occur when they see signs from above, including unexplained lights, sparkles, and colors.

As a psychotherapist, I was trained to believe that when people see something that isn't there, this represents a visual hallucination. In fact, I worked clinically with many people diagnosed as schizophrenic who told me that they were seeing things and people that I couldn't see. I can only speculate how many of my patients were actually seeing across the veil of heaven and were having angel visions, which we therapists inaccurately referred to as hallucinations.

Many of the angel vision experiences you'll read about here happened to children, which should come as no surprise. After all, children are less skeptical and less preoccupied with worldly matters, two factors that I believe hamper adults' angel visions. A 1995 University of Ohio study by Dr. William MacDonald concluded that children were statistically more likely to exhibit clairvoyant and telepathic abilities than were adults.[1]

I remember seeing sparkling lights as a child, and feeling deliciously comforted by their presence. The vision of what I now know to be "angel trails," or the electrical sparks radiated by moving angels, has been continual throughout my life. I always knew that, when I saw the bright flash of light or the Fourth-of-July-like sparkles, this was a happy sign validating my current choices. However, I didn't talk about these incidents until recently. Now that I am "out of the spiritual closet" with respect to my angel visions, I find that thousands of other rational, sane, intelligent adults also see angel trails.

If you're excited by the prospect of seeing angels, you'll enjoy reading the second part of this book, where I detail the steps that I teach to students who wish to have angel visions. Many people have used these same steps to successfully break through the visual veil, allowing them to see heaven's angelic creations.

Angels Come in All Shapes and Sizes

Between 72 and 85 percent of Americans believe in angels, according to various polls. One recent survey found that more than 32 percent of Americans said they have encountered an angel. One-third of the people surveyed for *The Skeptic* magazine's poll said that they've seen a "celestial being." Eighty percent of people believe in miracles, and one-third have witnessed miracles, according to a 1999 CBS television poll. So one could conclude that it is *normal* to believe in angels and miracles, and that seeing an angel is a relatively common experience!

But are all of these people talking about the same thing when they say they believe in "angels"? Everyone seems to have their own definition of what an angel is. To me, an angel is anyone who unselfishly helps us. When I talk about angels, I'm usually referring to someone in the spirit world, such as a deceased loved one, a winged Biblical type of angel, Jesus or a saint, and, of course, God.

Yet, angels also appear on Earth. Many of the stories you will read in this book involve meeting an opaque, real person who lends help or delivers a timely message. The person later disappears as mysteriously as they first appeared. This is the type of angel that Apostle Paul was undoubtedly referencing when he wrote in his Hebrew letters, *"Be careful when entertaining strangers, for by so doing, many have entertained angels unaware."*

From a purely technical standpoint, the word *angel* refers to a spiritual, nonphysical being with wings. The angels are messengers sent to us by our Creator to lend help, guidance, support, and protection. These angelic beings are recognized by all major Eastern and Western religions.

Deceased loved ones are usually called "spirit guides" because they have lived lives as human beings. The implication is that, once we have lived as a fallible human, we are a little denser and less enlightened than angels who have not lived a life on Earth. Of course, the spiritual truth is that we all are one with God and the angels. We are all God's perfect creations. However, in this dream of life, it appears that the angels are less Earthbound in their thinking, and therefore are more centered in a pure consciousness of love.

Jesus, Mary, the saints, and other great spiritual teachers are usually called "ascended masters." They stay closely involved with Earth's population, and are accessible to all who call upon them, regardless of one's religious orientation or practices.

Angel Encounters

Because apparition experiences and angel encounters have happened to so many people, considerable research and documentation is being conducted worldwide.

For instance, since 1998, Emma Heathcote, a theologist from Birmingham University in the United Kingdom, has interviewed several hundred people who have encountered angels.[2] Interestingly, those who were in the age range of 36 to 55 had the highest percentage of angel experiences. Heathcote categorized her study group as follows:

- 26 percent saw a traditional-style angel with wings.
- 21 percent saw a human form, which appeared and then disappeared.
- 15 percent felt a force or a presence
- 11 percent saw a figure in white.
- 7 percent smelled an unusual, unexplainable scent.
- 6 percent were engulfed by light.
- 6 percent heard a disembodied voice, or heard the voice of the angel or apparition.
- 4 percent felt or saw that they were enveloped in wings. (Other: 4 percent)

In this book, you'll read about a variety of angel experiences. The first chapter presents stories of people who have seen a winged being of light with their physical eyes. The next chapter tells about people whose angel experiences occurred during their dreamtime. As you'll read, these experiences are far from being "mere dreams."

Chapter 3 allows you to share amazing experiences with those who've had a mysterious stranger instantly appear, help them out, and then disappear without a trace. In Chapter 4, you'll read about these same types of strangers who appeared in the storyteller's life to deliver a timely or urgent message.

Apparition Experiences

Like the people you will read about in Chapter 5, I had an apparition experience, meaning that I saw and talked to my deceased loved one. It happened when I was 17 years old. My Grandma Pearl and Pop-Pop Ben were visiting my parents, my brother, and me, and I was very excited about it. They'd driven a long way from their Bishop, California, home to our house in the town of Escondido, just north of San Diego.

As a budding adolescent, I was in that stage where I preferred to spend more time with my friends than with my family. Pop-Pop must have understood this, because he insisted on driving me to a party that one of my best friends was having on a Saturday night. During the drive, Pop-Pop told me stories of his own teenage days. I felt a renewed closeness to my grandfather that evening as he dropped me off with a hug.

The next day, Pop-Pop and Grandma Pearl left for their drive back home. It had been a wonderful visit for us all. But about 6 P.M., the phone rang. I watched my father's body shudder violently, and he exclaimed, "Oh, no!" Something was terribly wrong. "There's been an accident," he told us. "Grandma Pearl's in the hospital, and Ben's dead." His words about Pop-Pop's death—"Ben's dead"—still echo in my ears.

My Mom, Dad, and brother seemed to go into a flurry of emotional upset. They were loudly protesting the situation, crying, and hugging one another. To escape my own distress, I went into my darkened bedroom and grabbed my acoustic guitar.

I absentmindedly strummed the strings, feeling terribly guilty that I wasn't crying about my grandfather's death. It wasn't that I didn't love him, but my honest feelings were that my Pop-Pop Ben was peaceful and that there was no need to feel sad.

Just then, a bluish-white light just past the foot of my bed grabbed my attention. There, standing in the middle of the light was my Pop-Pop! When I first saw the first *Star Wars* movie years later, the scene with Princess Leia projected from C3PO's stored memory reminded me of how my Pop-Pop looked to me. He was at once three-dimensional, and half of his original size, like a four-foot-tall hologram.

Although I don't recall my grandfather moving his lips, he transferred his thoughts to me with the same familiar voice he'd always had. His words, somehow telepathically transmitted into my mind, were, "You are right to feel this way [referring to my peacefulness]. I am fine." My guilt vanished, and I realized that there was no need for grief. Pop-Pop was all right.

Many of the stories in this book's two chapters on apparition experiences have similar themes, where a deceased loved one tells the living person, "I'm okay. Please don't worry about me." In the first chapter, you'll read about people who, like me, saw their deceased loved one with their physical eyes open. In the chapter that follows, you'll hear from people who interacted with a deceased loved one while dreaming. Just as in the angel dream chapter, you'll recognize the extraordinary nature of these dreamtime apparition experiences.

Paranormal researchers define *apparitions* by their features, such as their ability to instantly appear and disappear, with no trace of coming or going. Apparitions also pass through solid objects, walls, and closed doors. They also glide or float, rather than walk.[3]

Surveys in Great Britain and the United States show that between 10 and 27 percent of the general population have had an apparition experience, where they saw and interacted with a deceased loved one.[4] According to author, priest, and sociologist Andrew M. Greeley of the General Social Survey at the University of Chicago, nearly two-thirds of widows have had an apparition experience, mostly with their deceased husbands.

Greeley's research showed that the belief in life-after-death experiences is increasing, and that the majority of people now believe in the soul's survival. He wrote:

> Belief in life after death has become more prevalent in
> the 1990s than it was in the 1970s, according to data from

the General Social Survey. Roughly 85 percent of Protestants believe in life after death in every cohort. The change occurred among persons from minority religions and persons with no religious affiliation. The proportion of Catholics believing in the afterlife rose from 67 percent of the cohort born 1900–09 to 85 percent of the cohort born 1960–69. Belief in life after death among Catholics who graduated from college runs about 11 percentage points ahead of its level among Catholics who stopped their educations at the end of high school, and 16 percentage points ahead of Catholics who dropped out of high school.

Among Jews, this belief increased from 17 percent of the 1900–09 cohort to 74 percent of the 1960–69 cohort. Finally, the conviction that the human soul survives death increased among adults who have no religious affiliation (has risen) from 44 percent believing, to 58 percent.[5]

Those who have had an apparition experience say that it's not important whether other people believe them. They *know* that they've truly encountered the living spirit of a deceased loved one. However, they often don't tell other people about their experience because they want to avoid ridicule or skepticism. Yet, those who have had an apparition experience find comfort in the company of believers and those who have also encountered a deceased loved one. I believe it's time for us to "come out of the spiritual closet" and start openly sharing our apparition experiences. Only then can we realize how common it is. We can also benefit from the loving and transformative wisdom imparted by deceased loved ones.

Even though people who have had apparition experiences stand by the validity of their meetings with deceased loved ones, science requires additional ways to verify the authenticity of these events. Two ways that scientists "test" the experience is by noting when a person has received *new* information from a deceased loved—for instance, if a deceased loved one accurately tells you about a future event, or if you are told that someone has just died—and that was something you did not know up to that point.

Second, researchers look for group apparition experiences, where more than one person simultaneously sees the same apparition. Such group experiences have been reported with apparitions of Mother Mary for decades. In a study of 283 people who have had apparition experiences, two or more people saw and heard the same deceased loved one in about one-third of the cases. A similar study found that 56 person of the apparition cases involved several people seeing the deceased loved one simultaneously.[6]

Dreaming of Angels and Deceased Loved Ones

Is a dreamtime encounter with an angel or deceased loved one any less valid than a waking angel experience? My research and personal experiences show that sleeping and waking angel experiences are equally profound. For instance, my grandmother Pearl (wife of Pop-Pop) came to me in a dream two years after her passing. She was so real, so palpable, so audible. Grandma Pearl said only two words, but they still ring in my ears: "Study Pythagorus."

I woke up and said, "The triangle guy?" I quickly jotted down her words on the notepad I kept on my nightstand. My knowledge of Pythagorus was limited to high school algebra classes, so I wasn't even sure how to spell his name.

Trusting Grandma, I scoured the Internet and specialty bookstores for Pythagorean material. I learned that the ancient philosopher was a strict vegan vegetarian, and that he and his "mystery school" students would meet in caves to study alchemy and alternative healing methods. Among their discoveries were the vibratory patterns of stringed musical instruments. In particular, Pythagorus noted the mathematical formulas behind different musical notes and chords. The vibration of each tone was thought to hold a specific medicinal quality.

His vibrational studies were akin to the numerological work of ancient Egyptians, who devised systems that were the basis of Tarot oracle cards. I learned that each Tarot card was numbered, and that the number held a specific meaning. Each card's title and artwork also had unique vibrational properties. When a person asks a question and then draws a Tarot card, the vibrational rhythm of their thoughts and emotions would automatically attract a Tarot card with similar vibrational properties. This is referred to as "magnetic attraction."

Because my Grandma Pearl urged me to study Pythagorus, I ended up creating a deck of angel oracle cards, similar to Tarot, but with no negative or frightening cards in the deck. The cards have a life force of their own, because of the magnetic attraction that always draws the right card to answer a person's questions.

The dream also led to my interest in numerology. I learned that the angels often speak to us by nudging us, just in time to see certain number sequences on the clock, on license plates, signs, and other locations. I studied the meanings of the various number sequences that people often see, from their angels' guidance, and wrote a chapter on the number divination in my book *Healing with the Angels.*

You'll notice that many of the dreams recounted in this book have led to amazing consequences. In several of the stories, the dreamer's life was saved when an angel or deceased loved one gave an urgent warning.

One of the qualities that distinguishes mere dreams from truly psychic dreams is that psychic dreams tend to be especially vivid. In a survey of 229 psychic dreams, John Palmer of the University of Virginia found that 80.5 percent of the dreams were described as "especially vivid."[7] Psychic research expert Ian Stevenson of the University of Virginia School of Medicine concluded that the data about psychic dreams "suggest that vividness in a dream is a marker of paranormality."[8]

Some of the angel vision stories in this book also occur when the person is meditating or in the middle of receiving a healing session. To me, these angel visions are just as powerful and real as any other type of encounter. Once when I was working with a spiritual healer, I was in a deep trance. Suddenly, I saw a man's face in front of me. Although he'd died before I was born, and I don't remember seeing any photos or videos of him, I absolutely knew that this was my maternal grandfather.

My grandfather told me about some regrets he had about raising my mother. He said that his parental mistakes had deeply affected my mother's self-esteem, which in turn had negatively impacted my own self-worth. I felt a palpable and auditory "whoosh," as if years of emotional pain were being released from my body. The occurrence affected me in a profoundly healing way, similar to the healing insights experienced by the storytellers in this book.

Could It Just Be My Imagination?

One may wonder about the difference between a hallucination and a true paranormal experience. Researcher Bruce Greyson, M.D., studied 68 people who were clinically found to *not* be schizophrenic. He found that 34 of the people, exactly half of his subjects, reported having an apparition experience.

Ian Stevenson, M.D., quotes researcher D. J. West as giving the definitive distinction between a hallucination and a true psychic experience:

> Pathological hallucinations tend to keep to certain rather rigid patterns, to occur repeatedly during a manifest illness but not at other times, and to be accompanied by other symptoms and particularly by disturbances of consciousness and loss of awareness of the normal surroundings. The spontaneous psychic [now often called "paranormal"] experience is more often an isolated event disconnected from any illness or known dis-

turbance, and definitely not accompanied by any loss of contact with the normal surroundings.[9]

In my clinical experience, a hallucination—the type we think of as connected with mental illness—generally involves negative, frightening, grandiose, or paranoid themes. The person believes that the C.I.A. is spying on him; or that some agency, person, or entity is out to get him. Yes, people really do become targets of persecution; however, the type of angel and apparition encounters we are exploring in this book all have one common thread: The person involved improves in mood, outlook, or health as a result of having their angel experience. This is a rare, and even unheard of, result of a true hallucination.

Following a hallucination, most people feel insecure, as if they're losing their grip on reality. Following a true angel experience, people feel loved, secure, and saner than ever. "Everything now makes sense," is a common reaction following an angel encounter.

In addition, psychic researchers Karlis Osis, Ph.D., and Erlendur Haraldsson, Ph.D., note that during most hallucinations, the person believes that he or she is seeing a living human being. During apparition experiences, in contrast, the person believes that he or she is seeing a deceased loved one or ascended master.[10]

It's also interesting to note that Emma Heathcote, the U.K. researcher, studied the angel experiences of five blind people and found no qualitative difference between their visions, as compared to the angel experiences of sighted people.

Seeing Is Believing

In the process of teaching thousands of individuals how to see, hear, feel, and know the angels, I've learned a lot about how the human mind, the ego, the personality, and the emotions all impact the desire to interact with these heavenly beings. In the final chapters of this book, I'll walk you through the same processes that I've taught to audience members who have successfully had angel visions.

Whether your angel experience occurs in a dream or with your eyes wide open; whether you see an angel with wings, a helpful mysterious stranger, or your beloved departed relative, I'm sure you won't mind if I repeat my favorite quote from Apostle Paul:

"Be careful when entertaining strangers, for by so doing, many have entertained angels unaware." [11]

❯❮ ❯❮ ❯❮

Acknowledgments

Oceans of gratitude to Jill Wellington Schaeff, Emma Heathcote, Share International Media Service, Dr. Ian Stevenson and his staff at the University of Virginia School of Medicine, Father Andrew Greeley, Steve Allen, Steve Prutting, Corey Wolfe, Charles Schenk, Grant Schenk, Andrea Schenk, Bronny Daniels, Louise L. Hay, Reid Tracy, Jill Kramer, Christy Salinas, Jeannie Liberati, Janine Cooper, Jennifer Chipperfield, Tom Strapp, Arielle Ford, Bill Christy, and all of the men and women whose powerful angel stories grace the pages of this book.

꒰€ ꒰€ ꒰€

PART I

*True Stories of People
Who Have Seen Angels**

Author's Note: Certain individuals have requested that
only their first name or initials be used to identify them.

CHAPTER ONE

Adults Who Have Seen Angels

The Gift of the Angel Feather
by Kate O'Rielly

It was 1998, and I was in the emergency room with a diagnosis of pneumonia. All the drugs used to combat this illness were given to me, and I was sent home with strict instructions on the importance of bed rest and taking my many medications. When I left the hospital, I felt I should really be staying, but there were no available beds. It appeared that, because of my age and general health, I would recover quickly on a homebound regime.

That evening, as I tossed and turned, being kept awake by the sound of the vaporizer, I finally fell into a very deep sleep. At 3:33 A.M. exactly, I was woken up by some presence in my room. At first I thought one of the other sick members in my family was up moving about. When I turned over in bed, my heart began racing. There in my room were two very large bodies. As I focused my eyes, my mind kept saying, *How could something this large fit into my bedroom?*

The two figures quickly made me understand without words that they were protecting me as I slept. I knew that they were angels. One of the angels was a male who stood about ten feet tall. But how could a ten-foot-tall figure fit in my room (which only had an eight-foot-high ceiling)? His robe was a very lovely blue-gray, and he had a loving face that felt healing to me. The other angel was all white. Her energy was soft and nurturing. She reminded me of the angels I read about as a small child: half feathers and half human. I reached out to touch them, and they were gone. I fell back into a restless sleep.

In the morning as I woke up, I became very excited about "the dream" I'd had about the angels. When my daughter and granddaughter came in to see how I was feeling, I told them about my visitation by the angels. My daughter was old enough to be skeptical, but my four-year-old granddaughter was awed and delighted by the story. After the excitement had passed, my daughter helped me out of bed to visit the rest room. At that moment, my granddaughter started screaming with excitement and glee. As I rose from the bed, a six-inch-long white feather came with me, stuck to my feverish leg! The three of us didn't know what to think. I was very confused because there are no feather products in our home due to allergies. My daughter was speechless, and my granddaughter was dancing with joy because the angel had left a gift. She said she knew the dream wasn't really a dream because angels visit people at night all the time. Of course it was an angel!

I carefully removed the precious feather from my leg and put it on my bedroom altar.

The next night, I felt that I was getting sicker, not better. I decided that if I didn't feel better soon, I would call my doctor. At 3:33 A.M., I was once again woken up by the feeling of a presence in my room. I turned over, and there were the angels again! As I watched them standing across from me, the male angel asked if I was ready to go with them to heaven. In many ways, I was overjoyed to hear them speak, and to invite me to join them.

The angels said they were there to help me decide whether or not I would stay living in my body. I thought about the projects I was working on, and about the unfinished business in my life. None of those things seemed more important than going with the angels. The love and contentment that they emanated was so appealing, and I wanted more of it. All of a sudden, though, I thought of my seven young grandchildren. All of my friends had said to me that they were here for a reason, and I could be a part of that reason. If I left with the angels at that moment, I wouldn't have a chance to at least say good-bye to the children and receive a final kiss and hug. I told the angels that I wanted to stay on the Earth plane for now.

The angels told me that if I were choosing to stay, the only way I could remain alive was if I went back to the emergency room quickly. They disappeared as suddenly as they had come to me. As soon as possible, my oldest daughter took me to the hospital. As it turned out, the pneumonia had gotten much worse, and the doctors said that I had made it to the hospital just in time.

The next morning at 3:33 A.M., I woke up, hoping to see my angels, but they weren't there. I wondered if moving to the hospital had confused them. I was very sad to think that I might not see them again, and I wondered how I might bring them back to me. I realized I should have asked them more questions. I felt that I had missed an opportunity, and I questioned my decision not to go with them. I cried, feeling as if I were mourning friends I'd had for years.

My daughter and granddaughter came to visit me later the same morning. I hadn't talked any more about the angels since the morning of the feather. I was too weak, just focusing my energy on getting better. My daughter also had a lot on her mind, and I didn't want to burden or worry her. As we talked about my hospital experience, my daughter remembered something from earlier in the morning. She said she had woken up at 3:33 A.M. and had gotten a strong feeling about an important decision she was trying to make. She was very puzzled by the fact that she had received such an insight in the middle of a sound sleep. But now her mind was made up—after many months of struggle, she finally knew what to do.

I smiled. My angels hadn't left after all; they were still with me and my loved ones. To this day, I cherish the gift of the angel feather.

Embraced in Angels' Wings
by Joan Scott

A few years ago, I was taking care of my mother as she lay dying of lung cancer. Each day was so very traumatic, since I didn't consider myself to be a nurse-type person. I would tell the home nurse, "I can't do this," to which she would reply, "Yes, you can."

One night in bed, I kept repeating, "I need help." Almost immediately, I saw a huge gathering of angel wings totally surrounding and embracing me. The comfort and support I received, which let me know that I was no longer in this situation alone, gave me the courage and strength to complete my time with my mother.

Ever since my mother's transition, when I have times of challenge, I know I can always be surrounded by angels' wings.

❦❦❦

The Powerful Love of Our Angels
by Anonymous

I was working as an assistant teacher. We were all sitting in a large circle on the first day of school, participating in an exercise designed to get to know each other. We would go around the circle, and everyone would tell something about themselves. I had already had my turn, and as it came to the turn of a woman who was just a little to the left of me, I saw two angels.

As she began to speak, I saw at first what looked like heat waves rising above a blacktop on a sweltering day. The air above and around her seemed to move in this way, and then it turned into massive multiple colors, and then blue wings—two sets. I could then see the formation of beings attached. There were two of them coming down on both sides of her. If she would have raised her hand, her whole arm would have been inside them.

This all happened in a split second, and I did sort of a double take, and of course as I brought my conscious awareness back to what was happening, I could no longer see them. But I was so stunned. It was like those old *Bewitched* episodes where everyone freezes, except it was *me* who was frozen as everyone else continued talking. I couldn't hear a word they were saying. It was like I was just suspended in time for a moment, trying to catch my breath, still in the same vibration as these miraculous, beautiful beings; and even though I couldn't see them anymore, I could feel the tremendous love that the angels had for this woman.

I have only told this story to a few people, and the retelling of it does not do justice to the actual event. It is extremely difficult to re-create the feelings of this experience. In fact, as I sit here recalling it, I am moved to tears by the knowledge that we all have angels around us, and that they love us more than words can say.

❦❦❦

Angelic Coaches
by Terri Walker

My 11-year-old son, Steven, decided to play baseball over the summer, after playing soccer for several years. Most of the boys on his team had played baseball for years and were very good. Steven did pretty well, but he would freeze up at the plate and wouldn't swing at the ball. So needless to say, he would strike out a lot. We would take him to the batting cages, and he would do great, but during the game he would lose his nerve.

I was sitting in the bleachers watching my son play one day. Steven had already struck out twice and was getting ready to go up to the plate again. I noticed how his self-esteem was hitting rock bottom, and I wanted him to hit the ball so much. I decided to pray to his angels to help him hit the ball and get to first base.

Just at that moment, I saw an angelic being leaning over Steven's shoulder while he was standing at the plate. This angel looked right up at me and gave me a "thumb's up" and a beautiful smile. I couldn't believe what I had just seen! I looked around me to see if anyone else had noticed this angel, but no one seemed to.

The next moment, I heard a WHACK! Steven had struck the ball, and it flew between first base and second, straight down into right field. He made it to second base, stole third, and then ran home. The look of joy on his face was priceless! He was so proud of himself.

After the game, I told him about the angel, and he said, "I knew something wonderful happened because I felt that something was holding the bat, and I heard someone tell me to 'Swing,' and I did!" It just goes to show that the angels really *do* want to help, and that all you need to do is ask. Now, Steven talks to his angels all the time.

❧❧❧

Tara, My Healing Angel
by Robin Ann Powell

It was sometime in late November 1998 when a dear friend sent me Doreen's audio program *Healing with the Angels.* I was excited, since my health was going downhill. It seemed like all the healing methods I tried would only last for about six months. Prior to receiving the tapes, angels were merely pretty objects to me. I had them all over the house, given to me as gifts, but I had never experienced actually seeing them or hearing them or receiving a healing from them.

I remember when listening to Doreen's tape the first time that I fell asleep after about 30 minutes of listening, and nothing unusual happened. About three weeks later, my kidneys were hurting me. A year prior to this time, I had a bladder infection that I just couldn't shake. It turned into a serious kidney infection, and I had to finally turn to antibiotics to bring the fever down. The infection finally left my body. So, here it was December 12, 1998, and my kidneys were hurting me again.

My husband and I were not getting along that morning, so I asked him to sit down on the couch with me before I went to work. We got peaceful, and I had my eyes closed. Within a few moments, I saw this beautiful being. She had long black hair and was wearing a long white dress. She told me that her name was Tara and that she was going to put the backs of her hands—palms and fingers extended—on my kidneys all day. This was going to happen while I was selling shoes at the department store where I worked. She also told me that I was an earth angel. I opened my eyes in great astonishment.

I told my husband what had just occurred, and we sat there, stunned. Was this a real experience, or my imagination? I went to work with great anticipation, hopeful that Tara would heal my kidneys. Within a few hours, the pain was gone!

It has been over a year now, the pain in my kidneys has never come back, and I know that it never will! I'm sure that listening to Doreen's tape helped me bring my angel to me.

Angel in the Delivery Room
by Jacqueline Regina

I was with my daughter in the hospital while she was in labor. It was difficult to watch her endure so much pain, so I began praying really hard, asking for help and strength so that both of us could get through this. Just then, my daughter started to appear very sick and seemed to be looking at me for help. I didn't know what to do. I felt so helpless, so I prayed, "Dear God—help her!"

At that moment, I saw a very large angel appear by my daughter's bedside! It was so large that it practically filled up the whole room. This angel was looking down at my daughter, and then a few moments later, the baby started to come out, but the cord was wrapped around his neck! He was turning purple and black from lack of oxygen and wasn't breathing. Somehow, the angel communicated to me that he would be all right. I felt this message very strongly.

I shall never forget the beautiful angel who saved my grandson. I am so grateful that it was there to help us.

※※※

Comforted by an Angel
by Mary Rao

When I was 24 years old, I was living with my brother in a two-bedroom apartment. I had left the family home due to physical and mental cruelty on my father's part. I grew up very frightened. One night in the apartment I shared with my brother, I was scared to be alone. My brother was staying overnight with his girlfriend at the time, and I was afraid to fall asleep. I didn't go to bed in my room, but fell asleep in the living room with the TV on. But before I fell asleep, I remember talking to God and asking Him to help me though the night so that nothing would happen to me.

At about 3 A.M., I was awakened by a gentle touch on my forehead, and as I opened by eyes, I saw a beautiful spirit hovering in front of me. I could not make out the face, as it was not clear. Then it flew around the room and out the door. I was no longer afraid that night, and I believe that the spirit I saw was my angel.

Behold, I Bring You Glad Tidings!
by Jenifer Kennington

I was taking a shower one day, and I turned around to see this large life-sized angel. She was about six feet tall, and I believe that she was a female. She was glowing, with a light yellow color surrounding her. She had large wings that extended in back. Her hair was long and flowing and golden in color, and her eyes were a crystal blue, full of love and sparkling with joy. She had a ring of flowers in her hair, and she wore a long flowing gown that was white, yet glowed with an iridescent pale yellow color that encompassed her. She was barefoot. She had her arms extended out toward me in greeting, as if she wished to hug me as she talked to me. She was very beautiful and lifelike, and being so large and bright, I felt awed to be in her presence.

The angel spoke to me and said, "I give you glad tidings of great joy!" She then said, "You will have a baby boy!" This seemed impossible to me, so I assumed that it was a sign of a new beginning; however, six weeks later, I found out that I was nine weeks pregnant.

❧❧❧

Angel on the Highway
by Perry Koob

It was 1966, and I was 18, living in Los Angeles. I was out of school, as I had been kicked out for fighting the year before. I was pumping gas for work and had very few prospects. When my stepfather asked me to help my mother run a small farm in Missouri, I said I didn't have anything else to do, so sure, I would do it.

I gave notice, and two weeks later, I set out on a trip halfway across the USA, driving a Corvair that my stepfather had bought me for the trip. It was equipped with a one-wheel trailer loaded with some things I was to take back to my mother.

There wasn't a 55-mile-per-hour limit, and I was taking full advantage of that fact. I was doing 80 to 90. When I would put my foot on the brakes, the stop lights would make the tarp glow red. I was going down a very steep grade and had to keep my foot on the brakes. I looked in the rearview mirror, and I saw what seemed to be a woman sitting there on the trailer, smiling at me. I looked back to the road quickly. I then rolled down the window, thinking that the cold wind on my face would snap me back to my senses.

I looked back in the mirror, put my foot on the brakes again, and there she was. I could see her clearly in the tail lights, although the light was red. She was dressed in a long flowing gown, and her head was covered with a shawl. She was still smiling at me, and then she waved. I thought to myself, *Perry, you've finally gone off the deep end for sure now.*

I gathered as much of my courage as I could and pulled off to the side of the road just as it began a sharp curve. I put my head on the wheel, gritted my teeth, and got out of the car. As soon as my feet hit the ground, I fell down. It turned out that the road was all one big patch of ice! I got up, hanging onto the side of the car, and walked or slid my way back to the trailer. I lifted the tarp under the trailer, but there was nobody there. This shook me up, to say the least.

Just then, the moon, which had been behind some clouds, broke through and shone down on the desert below. The moonlight allowed me to see about ten crosses all in a neat row, marking the places where people had gone off the road and been killed. To this day, I look for that beautiful lady. I used to feel her beside me, but I no longer do, and I miss her being there.

How an Angel Helped Me Find My True Name
by Uma Bacso

I hadn't liked my name, Nancy Jane, my entire life—as far back as I remember. I tried Nan, NJ, Nancy, Nanny. Nothing felt like me.

One day, I decided to meditate on the topic as I stood in front of my bedroom mirror. After some time meditating with my eyes closed, I opened my eyes to do an open-eyed meditation. I saw a beautiful woman with long dark hair standing before me in the mirror. I asked this woman, "What is your name? What is your name?"

I heard her say, "Your name will have something to do with light." (At the time I had light hair.) I stayed seated for a short while after hearing that, then I proceeded to get dressed. One minute later, my body started moving over to my bookshelf, and I heard the voice say to me, "Your name will be in one of these books."

I felt my arm raise up as I was walking over to the bookshelf. My arm was now fully extended, and I picked up the book right in front of my hand. It was *Autobiography of a Yogi,* by Paramahansa Yogananda. I flipped through the book, and the name Uma seemed to stand out several times. I thought, *What a strange name.*

A few hours later, I went to yoga class and asked the teacher, "What does Uma mean in Sanskrit?" He said that Uma was the "goddess of the rising sun." I was taken aback for a moment as I remembered that the woman in the mirror had told me that my new name would be related to light. At that moment, I fell in love with my new name: Uma.

A Great Healing During a Time of Grief
by Jennifer Helvey-Davis

I was very close to my grandmother as I grew up. My mother was a single mom, so there were many times that I actually lived with my grandma while she helped my mom. You could definitely call her a stabilizing factor in my life, and she was always there for me. When I was 19, I moved back to live with her and my grandfather. One night, when I was 21, I had a horrible dream about a snake in my bed. It was so bad that I woke my grandmother up and made her come sit on my bed while I fell back to sleep. The next morning, I found her dead on the couch while reading a book. The event was extremely traumatic, and I was overwhelmed with grief.

While on my grass-stained knees visiting my grandma's grave site, I looked up to the sky and cursed God. I told Him that I wanted my grandma back. The sky I was looking into was slightly cloudy, and my eyes stung painfully from all of the crying I had done.

At that moment, this thing appeared in front of the clouds. It was like a starburst coming out from the center, yet it was gray, almost the same color as the clouds themselves. The starburst moved fast from inside itself and out again. I was certain that my eyes were playing tricks on me. Once on my feet, an image appeared out of the starburst, and it stole the breath from my chest. The being had long hair and a distinct heavy robe with a cord around the waist. The hands were stretched on the being's sides with the palms facing upward. I couldn't see a face, yet these majestic wings opened broadly from behind the back of the image I saw. They pointed straight up toward the heavens, and hands from the image were outstretched to its sides. From lack of breathing, I fell to my knees and whispered, "You are real . . . you are here."

This being had no face, yet it was the most powerful being I have ever seen. It was standing in the middle of the starburst and made me feel as if it had a lot of influence on my life. The wings were huge and pointed; they appeared solid and strong. The image was dressed in a long gown and had long hair parted in the middle. I was afraid, yet amazed at the same time. Although the being was hard to discern, I knew it was an angel. The wings and the hands made this fact very obvious to me. Now, I whispered, "You are an angel." As the tears spilled from my eyes, I could hardly believe what I saw. The angel acknowledged my presence and nodded its head toward me.

With miraculous speed, the angel's wings snapped back to its sides. They were fast and strong and made a loud "Whoosh!" as they did this. The noise frightened me, but I didn't move an inch. If this angel had been on the ground, it would have been at least seven feel tall, and the wings would have been even more enormous than that.

The situation was so overwhelmingly intense that I finally had to take my eyes off of the clouds. When I looked back, there was only the starburst shape, but no angel. I tried to look harder, but my eyes were so sore from all of my crying. I looked over at the place where my grandma was buried, and it seemed as if the grass on the plot made a shape. Some grass was darker in some places than others. When I looked really hard, I could see the shape of that angel in the grass.

I dropped the silk rose that I had brought for my grandmother onto the image of the angel, knowing that my grandma was in the mystical place that the angel had come from. Completely stunned by what had happened, I walked back to the car and scrawled a picture of the angel on a piece of paper. I left the cemetery with a strange feeling of calm and peace that I had not experienced since before Grandma's death. I often doodle pictures of that angel when I am feeling stressed or need comfort, and it always cheers me up.

An Angelic Vision of Motherhood
by Sharon Blott

At age 27, I was going through a very difficult time in my life. I was depressed, a six-year relationship that I had put all my hopes and dreams into had ended, and I had no direction. I remember saying to my mother that I felt dead inside, and I doubted whether that feeling would ever go away. I was in the middle of graduate school and had recently been told that I would never have children.

My mother insisted that I join her and my sister and brother-in-law on a two-week Mexican vacation in Cabo San Lucas, Baja California—her treat. At first I declined, but she insisted, and so off I went. The first week was fairly uneventful, but it was a welcome relief to be away from my surroundings.

However, during the second week, I had what I can only describe as a profound spiritual experience. One night, while on the beach during high tide and a full moon, the skies simply opened up above me, and I was engulfed in a glorious golden light that radiated a warmth and love that I have never experienced in this lifetime. I saw and heard the angels, and there was sweet music playing. The angels were beings of great radiance, with long white hair, and there seemed to be hundreds around, but only two or so that were really evident to me. The feelings they emanated were those of profound love and peace, and were intense and fulfilling to the very depths of my soul.

The most profound recollection was of children's voices saying, "Mommy, Mommy," and calling to me. It must have only lasted a second or two, but it felt like an eternity, and I wanted it to continue forever. I felt as if I was finally home. When I returned from my holiday, a trip to my doctor revealed that the condition preventing me from having children was gone. All my fears had disappeared, material possessions had little or no meaning to me, and I had a difficult time being within my physical body.

I yearned for that feeling of home. Eight months later, I met my husband, and today we have two wonderful girls, ages six and two. I will never forget that they are my miracles, and that ten years ago, in Cabo San Lucas, I was reborn and forever changed by my experience.

My story becomes even more complete when I explain that two months ago I received a community newsletter that was advertising property for sale in Baja California. My husband and I bought a parcel of land—my dream come true.

❦❦❦

I Met My Guardian Angel
by Dana R. Peebles

It wasn't a minister, youth leader, a close friend, or even a parent who strengthened my faith in God. It was truly God Himself. God really does work in mysterious ways!

While I firmly believed in angels, I had never actually seen my guardian angel—that is, until one night when I was awakened from a deep sleep and had the strong impression that someone was lying beside me in the bed. Since I'm single, I knew that something inexplicable was happening. Lying on my side, I was afraid to look behind me. So I waited for a while, listening to my own breathing until I got up the nerve to glance over my shoulder.

To my surprise, there was a male angel sleeping on his side. I was so overcome by peace and excitement that I woke up the angel. He opened his eyes and looked right through me with concern. I was startled at first, wondering who this strange man was in my bed, but then I soon realized that he wasn't there to hurt me, but to protect me.

This male angel was made of pure light—perfect in every way. He had shoulder-length blonde hair, nicely groomed, and he wore a white robe. He had a bit of a shine to him, kind of like he was in a bubble or something. I asked him who he was and why he was in my bed, and he said, "I am an angel sent from God to protect you, not to harm you, and I will guide you through your times of difficulty. Just trust me!"

I knew I must have been dreaming, and I finally dozed back to sleep. The amazing part of this is that I fell back asleep as my "guardian angel" held me in his arms. I felt at ease with this because most of my life has been filled with pain, fear, and abuse. I was and am honored that God would send an angel to watch over me.

ᴡᴡᴡᴡ

Angora, the Angel of Peace
by Dianne SanClement

Most of my adult life, I've prayed that my angel would appear to me. When I was 45, I realized that I could not spend another day working at a career that left me feeling empty. I fantasized about leaving, and wondered how I could do so. I was married, we had a mortgage, and all of the reasons why I should stay played on and on in my mind.

At this same time, I found myself waking in the night to the sound of chimes ringing in my ears, and I would hear an angelic voice whispering in my ear, "Dianne, you did not come to Earth to work and retire from the Boeing Company." I would lay there frozen, knowing in my heart of hearts that there was something much more important for me to accomplish. I knew that I had come here with a Divine plan, but I was scared because I didn't remember what that plan was.

The voices became louder, and I found myself reading books about angels. I decided to start journaling my thoughts and all of the messages I was receiving. It wasn't long before I knew that a power much greater than I was guiding me, and that I no longer had a choice. In order for my spirit to live, in order for my light to shine, I had no choice—I had to leave Boeing. The environment was suffocating my spirit.

On March 31, 1995, I walked away from my job, which no longer served me, without a clue as to what I was going to do. I prayed for guidance, and also prayed that I would learn to trust.

I began getting up each morning, journaling my thoughts, my fears, my joys, and whatever was on my mind. I could now sit quietly for as long as I wanted, and write. It was wonderful. It wasn't long before I found that I would sit for an hour and write, and that the information was coming to me via the paper I wrote on. I would go back and reread all that was written and be amazed. At first it startled me, just as the whispers in my ears had. And with time, I discovered that it was a joy, and that a relationship was forming with my angels. When the angels were done passing information on to me, they always ended with "Love and Light, Your Angels." I was never frightened by this experience, but I never told a soul.

A few years passed, and we moved to Camano Island, near Seattle. For the first time in my life, I was surrounded by trees, woods, and gardens. I had been in the city, surrounded by cement and tall buildings, for 48 years. I had always prayed that I would live in the country one day. I spent the first summer working in the yard with my hands in the dirt, and I loved it. I realized, as winter arrived, that I had spent five months in nature and for the first time in my life, I had made a connection with Mother Earth. My husband and I even built an area where I could meditate and be close to all of the creatures, trees, and the wonderful earth.

On July 1, 1998, as I sat in my peaceful garden reading, I noticed something in my line of sight. There, standing 50 feet away, was a woman dressed in white, with long golden hair that sparkled. She even seemed to glow, and the field around her body vibrated. As I sat looking at her, she said, "Hello, my name is Angora. I am the Angel of Peace. I have much information to share with you." With that, I jumped up, ran into the house, grabbed paper and pen, came back to the garden, and wrote down everything she said. Hours passed by the time she said she would have to leave me, but not to worry, for she would be sure to wake me at 4:44. I was to have paper and pen ready and write down all that she said. I kept our date, and we have been in contact ever since.

Now, there are times when weeks pass before I remember to write. But Angora, bless her heart, is always there for me. I find that I spend a good deal of time in conversation with her. I can ask for assistance, and she guides me each step of the way. Angora has taught me a lot about the universe, and she has given me the gift of understanding. She has given me the strength to do and try things that I might not have tried in the past.

I have only seen her in form that one time. I am aware of her presence, and I hear her in my head, and the biggest part of all of this is that I listen. I encourage *you* to open your heart and listen for that voice. The angels wait for your invitation. They love you. I invite you to trust and open your arms, and you will receive their love and guidance.

)€   )€   )€

CHAPTER TWO

Children Who Have Seen Angels

A Giver, Not a Taker
by Lee Lahoud

When I was 11 years old, my father killed himself, and my mother developed a drinking problem, rendering her emotionally unavailable to help me understand or deal with what had happened to us or to him. I had learned in Sunday School that suicide was the worst sin there was, so I was really concerned about what had happened to my father. Was he in hell? Was it somehow my fault?

The only place I knew to go for answers was to church, so I shared my concerns with my pastor. Yes, I was told, my father was definitely in hell, and what's more, I too was going to hell, as were my children, and theirs, for four generations. The sins of the father must be borne by the children, I was told. Someone must pay for this sin, and that someone was me.

I was devastated. There seemed to be no reason for me to continue to live, no hope, nothing. Why would I ever have children, knowing that they were condemned from birth? I went home, sat on the floor in my bedroom, and decided to die. Then I saw a light. At first I thought it was sunlight filling the room, but actually, there in the light, sitting cross-legged on the floor with me, was a very happy, smiling man. He had beautiful long, glowing hair. I was fascinated with his hair, and the fact that he was so happy! We had a conversation that, at the time, seemed to be the most normal and natural thing in the world. He told me I could die if I wanted to—that it was entirely my choice.

There was no judgment attached to this, no right or wrong—just consequences. Either way I chose, I really was okay. But I also knew that if I *did* decide to die, I would come back and be in that same situation, making the same decision, all over again. I was sure I didn't want to do it again, so I decided I would stay.

The angel then urged me to decide how I would live. I saw two distinct paths: that of a "giver to life" and that of a "taker from life," and I was to choose one. Again, there was no judgment in this decision. It was completely my choice. I was shown a vision of where each path led. I considered both, and I chose the path of a "giver."

I Know That We Are Watched Over
by Tammy

One night when I was a child and was sleeping with my big sister, I woke up in the middle of the night and looked out the door of her room. I could see a beautiful angel in white, floating at the top of the stairs. I felt that the angel was a female or was at least appearing to me as a female. Then, by the door, I saw a boy who looked like he might have stepped out of a Bible storybook. He was dressed like a young David or Jesus. He had black curly hair and was not looking directly at me, but *up.*

I've often wondered what this vision meant. Now, almost 30 years later, I think it was most likely evidence that my instincts and intuitions were and are correct: There are angels and beings who watch over us and communicate with us. I have never *felt* alone because I have never *been* alone.

From the Mouths of Babes
by Doreen Wetter

Bedtime was my two-year old daughter, Brittany's, least favorite time of the day. At night, she would beg us to stay with her until she feel asleep. This was very taxing on my husband and me. One night I was all prepared for a struggle from Brittany when she said, "Mommy, you don't have to stay here until I fall asleep—the angels will tuck me in." Brittany went on to describe beautiful people in long, shiny white coats. These beautiful people sang her to sleep.

ᴡᴡᴡᴡ

A Classroom Full of Angels
by Janette Rodriguez

My son, Matthew, had just turned five years old and was ready for kindergarten. I was concerned about him because I knew that he was clairvoyant and clairsentient.

In our home, we'd always talked of angels and God. We shared our visions and dreams, and we would see angels in our home throughout the day. My daughter, Faith, had gone through a few situations when expressing her spirit at school that led us to believe that many people are not willing to accept who they truly are. As a result, Faith shut down her gifts of clairvoyance and claircognizance. Children can be very cruel to one another, so Faith learned what *not* to express at school.

So, this was my concern for Matthew, because he is even more verbally expressive than his sister, which could have made him a target for ridicule. So I prayed continually about the situation.

My prayers were definitely answered! When I came to pick Matthew up from his first day of school, he ran into my arms, saying with excitement, "My teacher believes in angels, Mom!

And she wants to talk to you." I met Matthew's teacher, a very pleasant woman. As we went into deeper conversation, she mentioned how wonderful it was having Matthew in her class, and how funny it was that she also has six other students that talk of angels so openly. She said that this had never happened before, and what a wonderful blessing it was.

Now when I take Matthew to school each morning, there is music playing in the classroom to create a tranquil mood—his teacher plays CDs that have "Angel" in the titles. Matthew tells me that the class even has a special chair for the angels, and they all get to have snack time together!

Through the Eyes of a Child
by Allison Ralph

At the suggestion of a friend who is convinced that small children can see angels more easily than adults, I asked my two-year old son, Christopher, "Do you see the angels?" "Oh, yes," he said, pointing up, "they are up there on the ceiling." Needless to say, the hairs on my arms stood up! We do not attend a church and do not have any strong religious convictions, so angels were not a topic that we had ever discussed.

What a Child Sees
by Pamela Weber

Jessica, my six-year-old daughter, told me that the angels come to her for real and in her dreams. They come almost every night when she wakes up, and they sing her beautiful lullabies to put her back to sleep. One night, she said that she asked the angels where they go when they leave her room, and the angels asked Jessica if she would like to see.

When Jessica replied, "Yes!" the angels took her upward with them. She says that her surroundings became colored pink and purple and sparkly. She saw adult angels, kids, and baby angels there, and they were all singing beautiful songs. She said that they then brought her back to her room, and when the angels exited, they entered a bright light and went back up. She was so excited about this, and she looks forward to her meetings with them in her dreams.

I told her she was a very fortunate little girl, and that she should never let anything or anyone come between her and her angels.

Out of Harm's Way
by Anonymous

When I was five or six years old, I was awakened from my sleep to see a young man in a red choir robe with a red prayer book floating in my room. I screamed for my mother and father. The young man (I believe him to be my guardian angel) proceeded into my closet, and I ran down the hall to my mom and dad's room, where I stayed for the rest of the night.

Many years later, my mother and I were discussing the tear in the screen of my window that my brother and I used to climb in and out of. I told my mother that I always wondered how that got there. I knew my brother and I did not tear the screen. She said that someone tried to break into our house through that window the night that I saw my guardian angel. She didn't want to tell me because she didn't want me to be afraid to sleep in my room. Now I know that my angel protected me from harm that night.

CHAPTER THREE

Strangers Who Come from Out of Nowhere, Provide Physical Help, and Then Disappear

Stranger on an Icy Highway
by Susan Daly

A chain had fallen off of my husband, Clark's, car, and while retrieving it, he had slipped and fallen on an icy patch. After he managed to climb the hill to our house, Clark collapsed on our floor, writhing in agony. He had hurt his back during the fall.

I immediately called our HMO and asked for an ambulance to take him to the hospital. They said that they would be glad to send one, but if Clark had no significant injury, we would have to pay $500. Since I couldn't tell whether Clark was "significantly injured," and I didn't have that much money to spare, I decided to drive him myself, and my son, Scott, came along.

As we drove down a very busy stretch of freeway, Clark became nauseated, and I had to pull off onto the shoulder of the road. Finished with that, I began the daunting task of getting back into traffic, which was moving at a fast clip on the freeway. It was a very dark night, and as a space in the long line of headlights appeared, I began to maneuver into traffic only to find that I couldn't get traction in the snow! Scott opened the sliding door at the side of the van and tried to push us, but we sat with tires spinning, making no progress forward.

The empty spot in traffic had given way to another continuous string of headlights. I tried to move to an area where there might be more traction, but the van still didn't move! I put my head in my hands on the steering wheel and said, "God, I need help *now*!"

A moment later, a car stopped in the right lane of the freeway about ten feet behind my van. Its headlights were on, but not the emergency flasher lights that would warn other drivers about our presence in the slow lane. A long line of cars was stopped behind it. It was almost like a time warp, if you will, except that traffic continued to move in the center lane of the freeway. The road was slick, so for all those cars to just stop without accidents occurring was phenomenal. It would have even been miraculous if the pavement had been dry!

I saw a person get out of the car that had stopped behind me. He appeared to be of average height, dressed in pants (probably jeans), a short jacket, gloves, and a stocking cap. I couldn't see any facial features, since the lights from the cars behind him just allowed me to see a shadow. Somehow I knew that he was there to help my son push, so I gave the engine gas and focused on getting the van moving to a point where we'd get enough traction to drive on our own.

As I felt the van's speed increase, I told my son to jump in, fearing that I would have to stop again to pick him up. My concern about my son getting into a moving vehicle distracted my attention from the person helping him. With my window closed, shifting gears, and avoiding a guardrail of the bridge, I had my hands full and couldn't open the window to thank our rescuer.

Later on, when I asked Scott if he had been able to thank the person who had helped him push, he said, "What are you talking about, Mom? There wasn't anyone helping me push the van. I did it all by myself!" At age 15, Scott was convinced that he was strong enough to have pushed the van on his own.

So many times I've wished that I could thank the person who had helped get us back on the road, but I actually doubt that he was a person; I think he was an angel sent in response to my prayer for help. After all, it wasn't possible for someone to have seen our plight, stopped their car, gotten to the back of my van and pushed, and then returned to their own car in the time frame in which this incident occurred. How could all that have happened on a crowded, fast-moving freeway in icy weather, without an accident occurring in the process? The only possible answer is Divine intervention, an immediate answer to my short, demanding prayer.

It turned out that Clark had suffered a compound spinal fracture. It was painful for a few weeks, and he had to wear a back brace, but he's fine today. And for that, we once again thank God.

The Heavenly Nanny
by Catherine Lee

I have seen and spoken to my oldest son's guardian angel. We were living in Lubbock, Texas, at the time. Brandon was two years old and was very adept at opening doors, latches, and locks. It was a Sunday, and we were at church.

I was sitting on the couch in the foyer of the church because I was in my eighth month of pregnancy, and the Sunday School chairs were uncomfortable. The foyer had large windows on either side of a double door. The entire wall was plate-glass, covered with filmy curtains to let in filtered light. My husband was sitting with me on the couch when we noticed a woman approaching, holding the hand of a small boy. As she opened the door, we realized that the small boy was Brandon, our son. We had taken him to the church nursery for his class.

The woman had white hair and a very pale complexion. Her suit was white with tiny black piping. She carried a white purse and had on white shoes. She asked if this little boy belonged here at this church. For a moment, I was just too stunned to speak. She continued saying that she had seen him wandering down by the lake at the park behind the church and thought he might be in danger. Brandon would have had to escape through several doors and a latched gate to get off the church grounds.

I said he was mine, and she handed him over and went out the door. I realized that I had not said thank you and went out after her. She was gone. The sweet elderly woman had disappeared without a trace, just as mysteriously as she'd first appeared. Brandon is now 20 and a fireman. I hope his sweet angel is still looking out for him.

Rescuer from Out of Nowhere
by Sally Miller

I had something happen when my daughter was two years old (that was 28 years ago). I'm left-handed, and that day, my left wrist was in a cast. My daughter and I were leaving my mother's house, and unbeknownst to me, my daughter had a Lifesaver in her mouth. Suddenly she started choking on the candy, and there was no one around to help. So I just let out a scream for someone to help me, and almost immediately, a man appeared. He picked up my daughter, turned her upside-down, and hit her on the back. The candy popped out. When I turned to thank him, there was absolutely no one there.

The Angel Doctor
by James R. Myshrall

On December 22, 1995, at 11:00 A.M., Hazel (my mother), Beverley (my wife), and I were involved in a car accident. In this accident, there were two deaths, but there should have been four. My mother and the gentleman who caused the accident passed on. My wife had crushed her kneecap and received a large cut on her forehead. I crushed my face from the eyes down. I was choking, and drowning in my own blood. Within seconds, a mysterious doctor and his wife appeared. He came through the windshield of our car, pinned me down (as I was thrashing around due to a head injury), and cleared the blood away, making it possible for me to breathe.

This unknown doctor prepped me for the ambulance to take me the great distance to a better-equipped hospital. Through various channels, I've tried to find out how to locate this doctor, and I even tried through the TV series *Unsolved Mysteries.* But I've had no luck. I am unable to locate this doctor or even get his name. There is no mention of his name in the police report. The only conclusion that I can come up with is that he was an angel. I am alive and well due to this doctor (angel).

The doctors say that my mother was killed instantaneously. I believe that she had requested that I not be taken away from Earth at this time, as it would be too much of a burden for my family.

❦❦❦

An Angel to the Rescue
by Judy Garvey

I was driving my truck to get groceries. I took my usual route on the way to the main street of the city when my truck suddenly stopped. I drifted to the side of the road and was getting my purse to walk to the main road, which had several businesses where I hoped I could phone a road service.

As I turned around and reached for the door, I saw a man dressed in security guard clothes with a walkie-talkie coming around the corner, right toward me. He came up to my car door, asking if he could help. I said I was about to go someplace to call the road service. He said he could do that, and I heard him speaking on the walkie-talkie while I quickly looked in my purse for the roadside assistance membership card. When I turned to thank the man for his timely help, he was gone! I looked up and down the street for him, but he wasn't there! The tow truck came almost immediately.

I started thinking about the nature of the help, realizing that there were no business establishments in the area that would warrant a security guard, and also the fact that the man came from around the corner and headed right to me. I knew that I'd had a wonderful blessing from a very real angel.

๑๛๑๛๑๛

An Angel for a Grieving Daughter
by Carla Tederman

Seven years ago, my father passed away. He'd had three open-heart surgeries in the previous year. My father and I were extremely close, and every time he would go into surgery, he would tell the pastor, "I'm not afraid to die. The only fear I have is what will happen to my daughter Carla. A part of her will die along with me."

He was right. Two days after we buried him, I totally lost it. It was raining, and I jumped into my car and drove to the cemetery. I was screaming, crying, and started to dig up the dirt on top of his grave in the rain.

A lady walked up to me, put her arms around me, and held on tight. When I stopped digging, she sat me down in the rain on my father's grave and talked to me for three hours. She said that her mother was buried near my father. I don't know what I would have done if she had not come to help me. She gave me her name and her mother's name. A week later, I went to the office at the cemetery and asked how I could get in touch with her. They had no record of her or her mother. I never saw her again. I believe she was a guardian angel looking out for me.

❦❦❦

Someone Saved My Life Tonight
by Justine Lindsay

I was 18 and had just finished school (I live in Australia). Normally, this would be immensely exciting. However, I was awaiting my exam results, which scared the wits out of me. Even worse, I caught my boyfriend (and first love) kissing another girl at our prom, just days before we were due to go away on holiday together for a week.

That week's holiday was hell. We'd fight and fight and fight and then make up, only to fight again a few seconds later. It was awful. It came to a breaking point when he said some really harsh things to me, and I stormed out and headed straight for the beach. I've had a fairly rough childhood, and all of this was getting to me. Although I'm ashamed to say it now, the thought of killing myself was at the forefront of my mind. I went to the deserted beach, and I began to walk toward a huge cliff. *My way out,* I thought. I was hysterical, crying, sobbing, and wailing. I couldn't see anyone on the beach, but then again, I wasn't in any state to notice anyone else.

At that moment, I felt someone tap me on my shoulder. It was a man of about 25, well groomed, with translucent skin and beautiful blue eyes. He asked me if I was okay, but he transmitted these words somehow silently, because looking back, I cannot remember him ever uttering a word. I began to tell him everything—*everything*. We walked farther, me pouring my heart out to him all the while. We sat and I continued, telling him everything that had happened to me since the age of 12, when my parents had divorced. This man did not say a word. I kept talking, and he gently guided me back to the beach house that I was staying in with my boyfriend. We reached the trail that would take me off the beach and back to the house.

He stopped and turned me toward him. I realized that I'd been talking nonstop for more than two hours. I began to apologize, and I thanked him for listening, all in the same breath. I told him that I should go because my boyfriend would be getting worried, and then I hugged him. He still didn't say anything, and I remember thinking that this was a little bizarre.

I turned to leave, ran up the beach a bit, and then turned back around to wave good-bye. But when I turned around, the beach was empty. I walked back down the beach to where I had just stood with him and looked around. Nothing. I looked down, thinking I was going mad, and shook my head. When I opened my eyes, I saw that there was only one set of footprints trailing up the beach from where this man and I had walked. I felt really weird at this point and ran back to the house. I never uttered a word of what happened that day on the beach to anyone.

I have become more of a spiritual person because of this occurrence, and I continue to search for more meaning in my life. I speak to my angel all the time, and although he hasn't "appeared" again, I have never been as desperate as I was on that day at the beach since then. I get little signs every now and again, but usually only when I ask for them.

Overflowing with Joy
by Nancy Kimes

The year was 1980. It was an unusually hot day in the middle of the summer, a day I will never forget! I was very depressed. Nothing seemed to be going right in my life, including a relationship I was desperately hanging on to. My life had no plan, no direction. I was looking for a way out, so I asked God for help. I needed to know that I was here for a reason. I wanted to be able to help myself and others. At the time, that wish didn't look very promising. I cried as I spoke to God, as if He were standing beside me. Then there was a knock at my door. *Oh, who is that?* I thought. *Should I answer the door?*

The knocks continued. I finally opened the door with tear stains on my face. Before me stood a man with a bright smile, around 30, handsome, with a clipboard under his arm. He was wearing a long-sleeved shirt and dark trousers. His sleeves were curled a few folds. He said he was sorry to bother me but wondered if he could have a glass of water. I couldn't refuse him, as it was hot as blazes out there. I asked him if he would like some ice, also, and he said, "Yes, that would be fine."

As I turned on the faucet, the heaviness I had felt seemed to be lightening. He finished his glass of water, and I asked him if he would like some more. He said yes, with much appreciation in his voice. So I poured him a second drink, again with ice. This time I started to feel like something was filling up inside of me. I noticed that my mood, my depression, was lifting. I was feeling better! The man finished his second drink, and I asked him if he would like another. He was still thirsty.

So, as before, I started to pour a third glass of water. I experienced an overflowing of joy, and spontaneously thought of a beautiful Biblical scripture: *"Those who thirst after righteousness' sake shall be filled."*

Who was this man, and why was he having this profoundly positive effect on me? I suddenly wondered. He finished his glass and seemed satisfied.

He thanked me warmly and left. As I shut the door, I felt a peaceful inner certainty that my answers would soon come, that I had a purpose and I wasn't finished here. I dashed to the kitchen window to see which direction the man went, but he was nowhere to be seen. He could not have disappeared from my view that fast! Then, within the deepest part of me, I knew that he was an angel in disguise.

My life changed that day. A whole new world opened up to me—a world of love, forgiveness, listening to others, seeing myself through others' eyes, and having the ability to help myself through helping others. Now that I think about it, whenever something happens and I find myself completely overwhelmed, I feel an unmistakable presence within or around me that gives me the strength and courage to face the challenge and move on, knowing that I will be fully protected.

Heaven Helped Me
by Carol Pizzi

On September 14, 1995, while driving to work, I started to experience a tightening in my chest and pain that was going up in my throat. After passing right by the hospital, I decided to try to make it to the office and have someone take me to the emergency room. However, after driving a few more blocks, I started to feel very weak and had to pull the car into a deserted parking lot. This was all happening at around 6:50 A.M., and none of the stores in the strip mall were open. Just then, a man appeared, and I asked him to call an ambulance, as I was having chest pains and trouble breathing. I remember him going into one of the stores to make the call. The ambulance came and took me to the hospital, where they performed a cardiac cauterization. After finding a blocked artery, an angioplasty was done.

After spending time at home recuperating, I returned to the strip mall, trying to find and thank the gentleman who called the ambulance. Since I had seen him go into one of the stores before their opening hours, I figured he must work at one of them. All of the store managers told me that they were not open at that time of the morning and that no one of that description worked for them. I could not find my guardian angel, but I'm sure that's who he was.

Pushed by an Angel
by Birgitte Suhr

As a Danish teenager, age 16, I was in Poland for a holiday with my parents. One day we were visiting Krakow. In the afternoon, I was walking down the sidewalk among lots of people. I took a step into the street, but suddenly I was pushed back to the sidewalk by an old woman wearing a scarf, and in the same moment, a tramcar rushed by me. I would have been hit by it if she hadn't pushed me away.

Quickly, I turned around to thank her, but she had completely vanished. I am convinced that the old woman was my guardian angel. In my prayers, I have thanked her many times.

It Pays to Pray
by Anonymous

It was an ordinary spring day, and my husband asked me to help move our older Firebird car out of the carport area, as it was blocked by a hedge and was not accessible to the truck that would tow it to the shop. As my husband pushed on it, I was to steer it out of the spot. Well, as we were pushing and steering the car, I found that he was unable to handle the job as he thought. His back was strained, and I was trying to steer the car while seated in the car. I felt that my sitting inside created more weight, so I decided to get out of the car and help push, too. The only problem was that I could not steer the car and brake it as well. This was an enormously heavy car—a 1976 Firebird has a lot of heavy metal—and we felt as if this was unbelievably hard to manage. Just as we would get the car to a stop, I would jump into the car to brake before hitting my husband.

I started to pray in my heart, and I asked my angels to help me. As I was stating these requests inwardly, my husband was trying to push the car, which was going nowhere. Just as I was in the middle of my prayer, I looked up and saw the most interesting manifestation of my entire life. There was a beautifully tanned man running from what appeared to be the fence by my house. As I watched him running, I noticed that he turned, almost as if he were feeling his way toward the car. When his loving eyes of blue met mine, he nodded as if he were saying intuitively, "I am here!" He approached the car and started to help my husband push the car back. My husband was totally shocked to see this man helping, but the two of them managed to push the car back and into place.

I hit the brakes and shifted the gears to park. I noticed that the man, who had blond hair, blue eyes, and a beautiful golden bronze tan all over, began to shake my husband's hand and say something to him that I couldn't hear. That's when I got out of the car and walked over to see him turn and leave, running in the same direction that he came from, and basically disappearing from our sight.

Just as I focused on my husband, I noticed that his eyes were watering, and I asked if he was all right. He couldn't speak, but finally after a few seconds, he murmured that the love from that man had been so incredible. I asked him what the man had said. My husband turned his face upward to me. "He said, 'It pays to pray.'"

We never saw the man again, but we have never forgotten this amazing and wondrous occurrence.

※ ※ ※

CHAPTER FOUR

Strangers Who
Give Healing Messages

A Vital Message
by Carol A. Austin

One day, my friend Sandy and I went to Dayton Beach, Florida, for the weekend. When the time came to go home just before dark on that March night, I realized I had an upset stomach. (Looking back, I wonder if I might have had an intuitive feeling about the drive home.) Anyway, we got in the car, with Sandy at the wheel, and I immediately fell asleep. We were just outside St. Augustine when Sandy hit a steel signpost. I was thrown all around the front seat (this was before the seat belt law). Sandy broke her nose, and when the ambulance came, they had to pry the door open to get me out.

My shoulder had been crushed, my jaw was broken—along with my fifth lumbar vertebra, and the lower half of my body was black and blue. The second week of being in the hospital, a young lady who was close to my age came into my hospital room. She told me that it was vital that I sit up in a chair for 15 minutes, otherwise I'd never walk again. During this painful process, she helped me, rubbed my legs, and talked to me. She was so kind, nice, and pretty that I didn't think anything about her being there. Later, after she was gone, I asked the regular nurse who she was. No one seemed to know what I was talking about. I believe that this was my guardian angel.

⚜⚜⚜

Comfort from Above
by Maureen

I had recently placed my father in a nursing home because he was very ill and on a ventilator. At the same time, my husband was in the hospital for a kidney stone. I had been visiting him at the hospital, and I went outside to have a smoke (I have since quit smoking). I started talking to an elderly lady who was standing outside getting some fresh air.

After we talked and cried together, I said I needed to get back upstairs to my husband. The lady took my hand, said my father was blessed to have me, and that God would wrap Him in His loving arms. She told me to hang in there, saying that I was an inspiration to her. Then she said, "Nice to meet you, Maureen." I had never told her my name! When I turned around, she was gone and couldn't have gotten away that quickly, especially at her age. To this day, I know I talked with an angel.

⚜⚜⚜

God Works in Mysterious Ways
by Patrice Karst

I was driving on Interstate 10, heading west toward Pacific Coast Highway on a Saturday afternoon. I was listening to music, and my small son, Eli, was asleep in the back seat.

I was lost in thought when the car in front of me slammed on its brakes! I was going at least 50 miles per hour, and started the painful process of hitting the brakes hard in an attempt not to careen into them. But it was obvious that there was not enough time or distance. It all seemed surreal as I found myself heading for the car in front of me at a high speed. It was terrifying!

I kept thinking, *Oh, God, is this where I die? What about Eli? Oh, God, please no!* I crashed into the car with a great impact. After I hit, I was shaking uncontrollably and was afraid to move, lest I be confronted with the horror of seeing blood, bodies, and glass everywhere.

But when I summoned the courage to look around, instead of seeing a tragedy, I saw a miraculous scene. My son, Eli, was still asleep! I was completely uninjured, which, considering how hard I'd hit the other car, seemed utterly impossible.

As I was considering this unlikely situation, a dark-haired woman with a very thick and indistinguishable accent opened my door, and I stepped out of the car. She threw her arms around me and said these exact words: "We are all going too fast. You are fine. Let us remember to slow down." Then she said, "May God bless you!" and she drove off. I stood on the shoulder of the road in a state of shock.

My car was completely unscathed, yet I had just had a huge collision. Not only that, somehow my car was parked safely on the right shoulder, completely out of harm's way, even though I didn't drive it there! I never moved the car after the crash. I should have been in the middle of the freeway being hit, with cars swerving to avoid me.

Miracle? Angel? Call it what you want. I just know that the mysterious lady and that experience made no sense to me. All she said is that we're all going too fast. Quite a metaphor for this crazy, intense pace we've all set for ourselves. I got back in my car and slowly drove home. God was there that day for Eli and me—I'm certain of it.

An Angel in New York City
by Anonymous

I decided to follow my fiancé (who soon became my husband) to the New York area in 1995. We settled in an apartment that we could afford in a neighborhood in New Jersey. This proved disastrous. There were signs that this impending move was not necessarily a good decision. I was involved in a head-on collision before our move, and other disasters included having my car stolen the day I started my new job, and having men expose themselves to me on the various subway trains I would use to commute to Manhattan each day. All in all, my husband and I had our cars stolen four times within a one-year period.

Finally, my husband lost his job and couldn't find another one with comparable pay. He decided to move back to the Washington, D.C., area, which had a thriving job market. I remained in New York City until a job transfer came through for me. During this time, I lived with a friend in Manhattan.

One day a man approached me after I had parked on the street and loudly exclaimed that I was in his parking space. My friend who was with me told the man that it was a public spot on the street. The man became quite angry. Against my better judgment, I left my car there. My inner voice told me to drive away, but my friend convinced me that I needed to stand up for what was right and not let the guy bully me.

Later in the day, I returned to find that my car had a flat tire. Someone had taken a knife and had slashed the tire repeatedly. I cracked. I knew that this was the result of the parking incident, since the man had threatened violence when I left the car earlier that day. I drove my car, crying all the way, to a safe spot, and called a roadside service to assist me in replacing the tire. I was totally hysterical at this point. The city had finally defeated me, and I felt hopeless.

After calling for assistance, I carefully scanned the area from all directions to locate the service truck that was on its way. I had parked in a somewhat secluded location that I considered safe because it had open areas where I could see people approach. I believed that the guy who had slashed my tire might have followed me.

As I awaited the service truck, I heard a woman's voice behind me asking about my car. I did not see this person approach and was quite startled because I had been carefully looking in all directions. While crying, I told her the story. She was very comforting the entire time, while listening intently. She said that God would not have put us all here if there wasn't room enough for everyone, and that He would always provide for me, be it a parking spot or anything else. She also told me that I would soon receive a great blessing that would heal the entire situation with my tire.

At that moment, I saw the service truck approach. Within a second, I turned to thank the woman for being so kind, but she had completely disappeared! We were not anywhere where she could have hidden or gone into a building. A great level of happiness and comfort came over me at that time, and I truly believe that the woman was an angel. There is no other explanation.

The blessing that she told me about also came true. The very next day, I received an award for $50 from an employee recognition program. This was the exact cost of replacing the tire that had been destroyed. In addition to that, it boosted my self-esteem! A true miracle had occurred during a time when I thought nothing good could happen.

❦❦❦

Everything Will Be Okay
by Dorothy Durand

My mother told me a story about an incident that occurred to her when I was an infant.

Tragedy weighed heavily upon her. At age 22, she had lost her brother, her mother, and my father (who died at 31), and I was gravely ill. The doctors had a new therapy that had never been tried on infants. They gave me a 50/50 chance of success if she consented to the treatment. If she declined, I would surely die.

So, my mother signed the consent form, walked out of the hospital, and went straight to the harbor where she planned to drown herself. Everyone she had ever loved had been taken away from her. She believed I would die and that she had nothing to live for.

As she stood staring into the murky water, a black man who appeared to be a dock worker stood next to her. At first she was afraid because he was such a big man. It was a rough neighborhood, and women just didn't frequent it for fear of bodily injury. But then she thought, *It doesn't matter.*

He said, "Killing yourself is not the answer. Everything is going to be okay." My mother looked away from him for a few seconds and looked down into the water again. When she looked up, the man was gone. She scanned the area, but he had simply disappeared into thin air.

Everything *did* turn out okay, as I obviously lived. My mother had a special affinity with the angels from that time to the day they took her home . . . on May 18, 1999.

❦❦❦

A Heavenly Companion
by Karen Revell

I was heading to work one day, and my car broke down, so I walked to the bus depot and waited for quite some time. No buses going in my direction appeared. I needed to get to work, so I decided to walk.

Work was about four or five miles away and entailed my walking across a bridge. I have a major fear of heights, and this bridge was quite high, with very low walls on either side. As I anxiously walked across, I started to get vertigo. I felt like my body would twist and fall off the bridge. When I got near the peak, I was on the verge of hysteria. I looked back to see if I should turn around, but realized that the distance was just about equal. There was no one else on the bridge.

I turned to walk forward, and suddenly a man came from out of nowhere and began walking next to me. He said, "Don't be afraid. I'll walk with you." He told me that he, too, had once been afraid of bridges, and that he would help me across. We got to the other side, I said thank you, and he walked off. I turned to say something else, and he was gone.

❦❦❦

Ask and Receive
by Lauri H. Mustoe

Last year, I was diagnosed with a rare chronic degenerative disease called pollychondritus, which attacks the cartilage surrounding all the major organs—heart, liver, and kidneys. My doctor told me that I would "die a slow and painful death." She said that I should get my affairs in order, and that I would be spending a lot of time in the hospital. She informed me that as the disease progressed, I would need surgery to repair any damage that occurred.

Needless to say, I was devastated! I couldn't believe what I was hearing! I told myself, *It can't really be that bad, can it?* The first thing I did when I got home was to look up this disease on the Internet. I read one woman's posting on a medical message board in horror, which told how she had the same disease and had gone through seven surgeries on her throat just so she could breathe! I couldn't bear to read any more, so I turned off my computer and started talking to God. *What am I going to do, God? I need your help!*

The next day, I was driving, with only 15 minutes to get across town to my next appointment. If I hurried, I just might make it on time. As I approached the major intersection, though, I felt a curious change. It was as if time had slowed down. I stopped at the red light when something caught my eye. I didn't know it at the time, but I was about to meet my angel. The first thing I noticed was her big black hat with big black feathers poking out of the side. Her hair was black, too, and was piled up under her hat with loose pieces hanging here and there. She looked like someone out of a Disney movie—the bird woman in Mary Poppins—only with black hair! She carried a black bag that had an umbrella poking out of it. I smiled and thought, *What a neat lady!*

She looked at me and gave me a great big smile. Without even thinking about it, I reached over and unlocked the passenger door. She opened the door and asked where I was going. Before I could tell her, she was half in the passenger seat. She was a short woman, a little heavy, and it seemed difficult for her to raise herself up into the seat. I told her to take her time. She informed me that she didn't want me to lose the light should it turn green anytime soon. I just smiled, suddenly feeling as if we had all the time in the world. I wasn't even worried about making my next appointment! I truly felt that everything would work out.

The woman got in and told me that it was hard to get her 83-year-old body to move fast. She fastened her seat belt, turned, and looked deep into my eyes as I looked into hers. I swear it felt as if there had been some kind of connection made right there and then! I felt so at peace with this woman, like family. She introduced herself as Louise. Something about her energy made me feel happy.

She talked nonstop and told me all about herself and her family. I was fascinated as I listened. Then Louise got very quiet. She asked, "Do you know what my momma used to tell me?" She turned to face me, and with a very serious look on her face, she said, "You *have* not, because you *ask* not." It was as if a loud bell had gone off in my head and woken me up!

Louise pointed her finger at me, and with a very serious look on her face, said, "You got that, didn't you?" I smiled and said, "Yes!" With that, time and space went back to normal. The light turned green, and she told me to turn right. When we got to her destination, Louise told me to park across the street, saying she wanted to walk.

She said to me before leaving, "God bless you." She tapped on my ashtray and said, "The next time I see you, I want you to get off of these cigarettes because I love you, and I want to see your lungs pink and healthy. And I don't want to have to come back and dance on your grave!" I laughed and told her I would do my best. As I drove off, I thought to myself, *Wouldn't it be funny if I looked in my rearview mirror right now and she was nowhere to be seen?* I looked, and she was gone.

When I got home, I thought about what Louise had told me: "You *have* not because you *ask* not." I looked at the picture of Jesus I have hanging above my desk. I said, "I *have* not because I *ask* not. Okay, Jesus—heal me!" It felt good saying that, and I walked away smiling.

That night as I lay in bed, I asked God, *What can I do to heal myself?* I repeated the question, hoping to get an answer in my dreams. Right in the middle of asking, I was interrupted by a male voice. This voice was loving, caring, and soft. It said, "You're already healed." I thought, *Oh, okay, thank you. I'm already healed. Thank you, God!*

A couple days later, I went to see a rheumatologist regarding my pollychondritus. The doctor looked me over, asked me a lot of questions, and then told me, "You don't have pollychondritus. I don't know what the other doctors saw. From their description, it sounds like you once had this, but now I can't see any evidence of the disease at all."

I just smiled all the way home! I thanked Louise in my heart. She taught me something very valuable: All you have to do is ask—you *have* not because you *ask* not!

❧❧❧

The Praying Doctor in White
by Lynne Starr-Post

I felt drowsy, but my mind was as active as a seething volcano. The injection that was to relax me did nothing. My eyes were sensitive to the stark white walls reflecting the extremely bright lights. Tears rolled down my chilled cheeks. It seemed that it was time for my death, offering me liberation from pain and prescription drugs. My children's little faces appeared in my mind's eye. Oh, God! I might never see them again, and I knew that! It was part of the risk I agreed to. My lawyer drew up the legal guardianship papers. My husband and my sisters finally agreed upon all of the legalities.

At that moment, thoughts of my own death were realistic and desirable. In fact, it would be a welcome embrace. My last surgery had been less than a month before, and five months of chemotherapy had left me almost lifeless. At last, my eyelids seemed heavier, and my thoughts slowed down. My doctor's rippling voice startled me awake. When my fluttering eyes were finally open, I saw my doctor and his associate. Simultaneously, they yelled for someone to remove my nail polish, "Immediately!"

"Yes, doctors," a female voice responded tensely.

I could feel the pressure of an icy-cold compress on each finger, and at that very instant, I finally felt extremely drowsy. "Now," said my doctor.

"Now," replied his associate.

"Lynne, you will be going to sleep now. Relax," my doctor instructed.

"Lynne, start counting back from 100," another voice commanded.

"Okay," I said. "100, 98, 97, 89, 63 . . . 33 . . ."

"Lynne! Wake up! Lynne! Can you hear me?" a disturbing voice shattered my sleep.

"Yes," I barely whispered.

"Lynne, you are in the Post-O.R. I.C.U. area."

As her voice trailed off, I felt a sense of relief, a sensation beyond my recognition. *My God, it is warm and dark all around me,* I thought. The velvety-warm space soothed away all of my pain. Finally, I was free. It felt so tranquil—what a wonderful experience. A gentle influence moved me along the black space. I was not afraid, nor did I resist. All I wanted was more of the quiescent sensation, and freedom from suffering and anguish. The realization of death, my death, overcame me. My own death was there to comfort me, and finally I was ushered farther into the mysterious black passageway. A mild air flow supported my body, and I could feel myself swirling in a backward motion.

"How grand it is," I sighed as I surrendered to ecstasy. No, oh no! I could hear the doctors calling to me from very far away. That peaceful journey didn't last very long.

My doctor yelled my name, over and over. "Come on, Lynne. Breathe! Breathe!" Someone sat me straight up and was punching or pounding me on my back.

Why are they doing this to me? Don't they realize I want to remain dead? I want to be dead! I'll just pretend I don't hear or feel them disturbing me. Suddenly, though, death released its grip on me. My wonderful protective shelter had dissolved, and it was now beyond my reach.

"Lynne, pray, pray," a soothing voice uttered.

My mind searched for the words. I tried to think of a prayer. "I can't remember the words," my voice choked out hysterically.

A hypnotic voice whispered to me, saying, "Hush, hush, I'll help you pray. Our Father who art in heaven. . ." Then I started to pray along with him, and we finished the prayer together. I experienced a protective shield separating me from all of my fears. His warm hand gently stroked my arm and tenderly patted my hand. My eyelids fluttered as I slowly opened my eyes. The praying doctor was a stranger to me. His handsome face and his gentle smile seemed to welcome me home. Death was no longer an option. I wanted to recover—I wanted to be with my family! The doctors were still poking at me, then they gave me an injection.

Unconsciousness overpowered me immediately. Three days later, I was strong enough to be moved back to the intensive care unit, where I started asking questions about the praying doctor in white. Disappointment enveloped me each time I was told, "Sorry, I don't know him." Fretfully, I waited for my doctor.

When he arrived, I impatiently started to question him. "Who was the other doctor? I want to see him. I want to talk with him." My cracking voice squeaked.

"You mean my associate?" he searchingly asked.

"No! The other doctor—the one who helped me pray!" I responded quickly.

"There was no other doctor, Lynne. Just my associate and myself," he said.

"Yes, yes, the doctor who helped me pray, the doctor dressed in white," I excitedly blurted out.

"Lynne, no one prayed with you, and as a matter of hospital policy, only greens are allowed to be worn on the surgical floor."

We never spoke of the incident again. My recovery was slow and tedious. Finally, the months turned into years, and I almost forgot about the entire occurrence.

That experience was at the Presbyterian Medical Center in New York City in 1993. I *did* have cancer and have been cancer free for all of these years. I know I owe part of my survival to the praying doctor in white.

Meeting My Angel
by Cammy Rosso

I attended Doreen Virtue's workshop here in Calgary, Canada, in October 1999. In the workshop, we were taught how to ask for our guardian angels' names. I discovered that my angels were named Teresa and Walter.

Two months later, on December 17, I had the most amazing encounter. I was working on a project at a Seniors' Drop-In Center for a few hours. I was chatting with an elderly lady when a man walked in and sat down. We began talking, and he told me that he'd had several visits from his wife after she passed on, and that he thought she was trying to give him a message. I told him that I believed in angels, and he responded to me by saying, "I know you do!"

I felt so comfortable talking to this man that I'd just met. He was so warm and caring and understanding. Before I knew it, I was telling the man how my husband has been out of work since last March and how tough it was for us to support our two boys.

He just sat and listened, and at one point he put his hands on mine and told me, "Everything is going to be okay; it's all going to work out for you and your family. Keep doing what you're doing and keep the faith, and things will get better. I know that it's a struggle right now, but it will work out, and you will get through this."

I had this feeling of peace that everything really was going to be okay as he spoke to me. Then the man said, "I'm going to tell you something, and you will know what I mean; you will understand what I say to you." He then told me that he loved me!

At this point, I felt like the whole world had stopped—just like in a movie—and I was the only one there in the room. I asked him, "What's your name?" To my amazement, he told me that his name was Walter! At that exact moment, I had no doubt in my mind that I was sitting there face-to-face with my angel! I also had this most unreal feeling, like a thousand shooting stars going through the top of my head right out my toes. I can't even begin to explain the love and warmth that I felt. I told him about the workshop and that my angels' names were Teresa and Walter. He smiled, and said to me, "Well, I guess we need to meet Teresa." I told him that I wanted to come back and visit again.

He told me not to worry and that we would meet again. Walter then took my hands, and again told me that everything was going to be all right and not to worry. He told me again that he loved me, gave me a big hug, and kissed me on my left cheek. He told me to have a Merry Christmas with my family and friends, and he turned around and walked out of the room.

I stood there for a few moments trying to take in every moment. I realized that the woman sitting at the table had gotten up during some point and had walked to the other end of the room. As I sat down, she walked back to the table and joined me. I said to her, "That man was so amazing and kind. I want to come back and visit him again."

She looked at me and said, "Yes, he seemed very nice. It's funny. I've volunteered here every day for the past three years, and that's the first time I've seen him here!"

❦❦❦

Dancing Angel Boy
by Jill Wellington Schaeff

The first time I heard the song "Hands," by pop singer Jewel, the words leaped from the radio, mesmerizing me with their wisdom. One line in particular, which referred to the fact that kindness was all that mattered, squeezed my heart. Now, every time I hear the song, my physical surroundings blur, and the spiritual message takes over my very soul.

That's what happened in November of 1999, only the words didn't flow from the radio. My husband and I are Cub Scout den leaders, overseeing a rowdy group of six second-graders, including our son, Mark. We were asked to supply a Christmas ornament project for at least 50 boys at the monthly pack meeting. The boys would move from table to table, making the ornaments from eight different dens, then deliver them to various nursing homes in December.

Our pack has 88 Cub Scouts, and it was also our den's month to create a neckerchief slide project for the month of November. The inspiration came early one morning in a dream. I clearly saw the project laid out before me—a little ear of Indian corn, popcorn kernels glued to a corn-shaped piece of cardboard with straw poking out the top. It was adorable! I jumped out of bed and headed straight to the kitchen to duplicate the project from my dream.

I spent the entire day experimenting with food coloring to get the exact hues for Indian corn. It took hours to mix the colors, blend the corns, and measure them into tiny plastic bathroom cups, one for each boy in our Cub Scout pack. My hands cramped as I painstakingly cut out 88 cardboard corn stalks and glued the straw on top. I then placed each one into a cup of popcorn kernels so that every boy would have a ready-to-make kit. Then he could glue on the kernels and complete a slide for his uniform's neckerchief.

I was proud as my family helped me carry the projects into the school gym and laid them out. Our long table was immediately surrounded by whooping boys from all the different Cub Scout packs, drawn to our neckerchief slide project.

"Look at these neat little corns," I heard them saying.

Little hands reached for the boxes in front of me, plastic cups tipping over and spilling. "I have just enough for each boy in our own pack," I said, my mind flooding with frustration. What seemed so orderly in my house was now chaotic. Finally, the pack leader saved me by announcing that each boy must rotate from table to table. Our table remained the most crowded, with boys vying to make the little Indian corns.

As my husband and daughter guided the boys through the ornament project, I struggled to make sure we had enough corn projects. "Honey, you only need *one* cup of popcorn. Try not to spill your cup, that's all I have." I was definitely feeling stressed.

During this confusion, a little boy danced over to me. Dressed in a long-sleeved plaid shirt, instead of the bright blue-and-gold Cub Scout uniform, the child appeared either Indian or Hispanic. "I want to make the little corn," he said, his brown eyes like full moons.

"Honey, you will make a project with your pack."

"Please, I want to make the little corn," he pleaded.

I felt overwhelmed with so much chatter, plus parents and adults vying for my attention. Losing my patience, I asked, "Where is your Cub Scout pack?"

He stared me right in the eye and said, "I don't have a pack." The answer was vacant, confused. Kneeling down in front of him, I firmly told him that I only had enough corn projects for the Cub Scouts, but that if he could bring me his pack leader, he could do the project. With that, he danced away, twirling around and around. I was relieved that his pack leader would deal with him.

That's when it happened. Within my head, louder than the lively din echoing off the cement walls, I heard Jewel singing the words from her song about kindness being the only thing that matters. My heart suddenly swelled with love and remorse. As little boys tugged on my sleeve, impatient for me to demonstrate the corn project, I rose from my seat, my eyes brimming with tears. "Excuse me, I need to do something."

I quickly made my way through the crowd, searching for the dancing boy with the heavenly brown eyes. I wanted to find him and invite him to make a corn slider, just as he'd asked for in his simple, sincere request to me. I thought that surely the little boy would stand out in the crowd, with his plaid shirt among the sea of blue and gold.

But he was nowhere to be seen. I walked from table to table, my eyes searching each face. I started to quake, my eyes scanning the length of each table in search of the dancing boy. He was not among them. Where was he? At that moment, I noticed a table with a group of physically and mentally challenged Cub Scouts. Like a former Scrooge who'd had a huge awakening of the heart, I announced, "I want all these boys to come to my table. I have a project waiting for you."

Precious eyes lit up, and parents delighted in helping the boys with various physical challenges get across the crowded room. I seated the eight boys around the Indian corn project, and watched in awe as they carefully glued the corn to the cardboard.

My heart sang with joy the rest of the evening, as the boys slowly completed their projects. Just like the fish that multiplied, my corn project seemed to do the same thing. After all the boys had made their neckerchief slides, I still had several left over.

I continued to scan the room for the dancing boy, but he had disappeared. I know now that he was an angel, sent by God to teach me a tremendous lesson about kindness. The experience ignited a change in me. Whenever I feel frazzled and impatient over life's little stresses, I sing the inspiring words from Jewel's song to myself.

❦❦❦

A Messenger from Above
by Kimberly Miller

The first time I realized that I'd encountered an angel was in 1985 when my grandmother had died suddenly from heart failure. She had been on dialysis for about five years, and during one of her treatments at Henry Ford Hospital in Dearborn, she'd had a major heart attack. She was rushed to Beaumont Hospital, and my father called me to tell me she was there.

Before I could even leave the house, my father called again and told me she was gone. I was very close to my grandmother and was devastated. I was extremely upset and concerned that she had died alone.

We were at the funeral home for visitation in Taylor, Michigan, and the oddest thing happened. A Dominican nun (these are the nuns that taught at the Catholic school I had attended as a child) approached me. She touched my hand and said to me, "I was with your grandmother when she died. She told me to tell you that she is okay now and she knows how very much you loved her." I was so surprised and was speechless for several minutes. I turned around to thank the nun, and she was gone.

I asked my brothers and my father if they had talked to the nun, and they looked at me strangely and wanted to know what I was talking about. Nobody in the room that day had seen her, let alone talked to her. I realized then that the angel had come to calm my fears about my grandmother dying alone, and to reassure me that my grandmother knew how very much I cared.

❦❦❦

My Fear Was Healed
by Helen Kolaitis

In the summer of 1996, my son Michael had a great summer vacation, which he desperately needed after enduring three open-heart surgeries in May of that year. He was doing great, until the fall came. We went to the doctors, and they told me that Michael needed to have another operation in September. I was devastated and went into a depression, feeling suicidal. The doctors medicated me.

Three days later, my best girlfriend insisted that we go to a local bagel shop with Michael and her young daughter. The shop was all glass, and had only one door leading in and out of it. We found a table in the back, where Michael and I were facing away from the other customers. At that moment, a woman came up behind us and put her hand on Michael's right shoulder. She said, "He sits there with such great strength."

Then the woman asked my son's name. When I replied, "Michael," she said, "Of course! Michael, the archangel." I noticed that the elderly woman had blondish-gray hair. She was wearing an old brown coat, and a gold ring with a religious symbol. She then told us to have a great day as she prepared to leave our table.

We watched her turn around and leave, but we never saw her go out the door or leave the parking lot! It was like she just vanished into thin air! After that moment, I took no more drugs. I was happy, and had no more fear of Michael dying. That December, Michael had his operation. We went through it with great strength, and all went well. I see now that the elderly lady was an angel, sent to give me strength and the will to live.

An Angel in Disguise
by Cheryl Cash

A few years ago, I decided to leave the profession of waitressing and become a legal secretary, so I started going to evening business school. Since my school and work were both downtown and the parking rates were too high for my income, I took the bus to and from work.

One evening as I sat at the bus stop, I noticed a tall, thin black man. He had a cardboard box and a restless way about himself. He seemed to try to make himself comfortable on the bench, but fidgeted a lot and would open and close this box over his head. Everyone who was there got off the bench and stood at the curb to avoid being near this man. And it seemed that as people snickered to each other and would look back at him, his behavior became more exaggerated. He put the box over his head and started singing some strange song at the top of his lungs. Then he would peek out from his box and look around, fuss a little more, and go back into his box and sing some more. He reminded me so much of a little boy looking to see who might be watching him. The man worked his way over to my bench, where I waited for the bus to go home.

When he stopped fidgeting and playing with the box over his head, noticing that I was neither snickering nor moving, he sat still. Then he looked at me, and I looked at him, smiled, and said, "Hello." He said, "Hello" back. And for the remainder of my wait for the bus, we sat silently, occasionally looking at one another and lightly smiling. The silence was our conversation. I said good-bye as I boarded my bus, and he also said good-bye.

The following night after work and school, the odd man arrived again and sat at the opposite end of my bench. I said hello, and he said hello. Again, we sat there with the silence as our conversation and the occasional glances and light smiles. Again, my bus came, and I said good-bye as I boarded my bus, and he nodded.

That evening, I thought even more about him and what I might be able to do for him. I began to think of him throughout the day intermittently. He took me away from my own personal concerns, and I think that was a good thing.

He was there at my bus bench every evening thereafter. I began to study him, and it occurred to me that he was quite a beautiful person. He had the smoothest skin, like brown satin, and his fingers were long and tapered, with very clean fingernails. He wore a ski hat that looked ragged, but his face was smooth and unlined. He had a beautiful, long Roman nose that was slender and aquiline. His eyes were deep and dark, and the whites were also very white and clear. He was wearing ragged clothes, but not one single part of him looked worn or dirty. He was absolutely flawless.

As the days went by, I felt that this man without a name was somewhat of a friend to me, and I wanted to do something for him. So, one night I offered him some money. He looked stone-cold at me, and seemed irritated. I offered to buy him food at a nearby restaurant, and he looked even more irritated. He said no firmly, shook his head, and then gave me the cold shoulder. What did I do wrong? Did I offend this man by offering charity? I deduced that he just wanted to be treated like an ordinary person.

Sadly, my silent friend never appeared again, and I felt so bad. Soon, though, I got so busy with work and school that I forgot about him. One evening I got out of school extremely late at night and sat at the bus stop, feeling vulnerable. Instead of the people I'd normally ride the bus with, the bus stop area was crowded with people who seemed up-to-no-good. I could not see any police officers, and there weren't many buses or cars driving by.

Soon, a man whom I had seen lurking in an alleyway approached my bench and tried to engage me in conversation. He gave me a very creepy feeling and asked way-too-personal questions such as, "What bus are you taking, where are you from, where do you live?" I answered his questions vaguely, and when he asked me if I lived alone, I turned and flatly told him to leave me alone and that I no longer wished to talk with him. He left, but I noticed him behind me watching me from a doorway with his hand in one of his pockets. It was frightening, and I could not find a single cop on the street to ask for assistance. I pulled a pen from my purse, holding it like a weapon, and started praying to Mother Mary and my angels to intercede.

Shortly after I pulled out my pen and began praying, out of nowhere, my silent friend appeared and sat on the bench opposite me! He said hello, and with considerable relief, I said hello in return. I was so happy to see this friend who had disappeared for a while that I completely forgot about any sense of danger. My bus came, I said good-bye, he nodded, and we both watched each other from the bus window as it departed.

From that moment on, he was always there at my bench, and I never offered him anything else but hello and good-bye and some light smiles that seemed to say everything that really matters in this world.

I started working in a new area of town, and transferred to a school campus in the same vicinity. That meant no longer taking the bus, and it also meant that I could drive my car to work and school.

My last night downtown, my friend arrived, and we said our usual hello's, accompanied by the silence. This time he looked at me and he said, "You look like you have a world on your mind. Would you like to talk?" I was taken aback by this change in flow, and I thought, *Okay, I'll talk with him.*

As I spoke with this man, his face filled with a sense of peace and contentment, and it was as though my words were lulling him to sleep, like a small child listening to his mother tell him a bedtime story. My bus came, and I said good-bye, and I knew that this was the last time we would sit together. We silently watched each other through the bus window as it moved on.

Soon after, I told a good friend about this man; we both thought I could bring him an old but very warm blanket—a way of giving him something. Well, I packed that blanket and went up and down that street looking for him. I knew where he could usually be found, but I couldn't find him anywhere. I tried all different hours and days, and no, he could never be found so that I could give him the blanket.

I wrote about this man a couple of years later in an English class because of how deeply he touched me. We were engaged in a group writing assignment where we each presented our different points of view on homeless people. It was in this class that a couple of women from my group approached me and said, "Don't you think that man was your angel? We think so; our skin has goose bumps from hearing that story."

I had read some books on angels, but I'd never put two and two together. But now, thinking back to how beautiful his features were, his long Roman nose, his satiny look beneath the rags, the way he appeared when I felt in danger, and the way he sat with me—yes, I believe he was an angel, sent to give me comfort and protection in a time of loneliness.

Bless Her Heart
by Susan Sansom

In 1994, at the age of 44, I awoke at 4:30 A.M. to incredible chest pains. The pains were so severe that my husband called an ambulance. Several paramedics arrived, and they confirmed that I was having a heart attack. The paramedics shared this news with my husband, but they all decided not to tell me. En route to the hospital, I told the paramedics that I felt like I was going away, and that they sounded strange and distant. At that moment, I let go and died.

I heard the paramedics frantically saying that I had flat-lined. I watched one of the paramedics, a tall blonde woman, scream, "You're not doing this to me!" as she slammed me in the chest. I saw her hit me and was somewhat surprised that I didn't feel it! I was revived and was code red at the local hospital.

I was going in and out of consciousness in the emergency room, with three doctors and several nurses in attendance. I was administered Beta Blockers, and the doctors told my husband to call my family members so that they could come and say their final farewells to me. As the Beta Blockers coursed through my system, I felt cold, the deepest and most bone-chilling cold I have ever experienced.

Still uninformed about the severity and details of my condition, I started talking to a nurse. She had the sweetest smile and held my hand. She was of medium build and looked matronly. She didn't wear a regular nurse's uniform, which, in my confused state, I did not question. She told me that I'd indeed had a heart attack, but that it was over and I would never have another one. This news greatly eased my mind, and I drifted off to sleep.

When I awoke, I was in the hospital's intensive care unit, and the doctor asked me to decide which hospital I would like to use for my heart surgery. He also stated that I was to undergo cauterization at 1 P.M. that day and that I was in a very bad way. Normally they scheduled such procedures for the following day, but as he explained, I was likely to have a fatal heart attack at any time. A helicopter would soon land on the hospital roof and transport me for immediate surgery to a town 30 miles away.

To say I was confused by this news was an understatement, since the nurse had assured me that I would never again have a heart attack. At 1 P.M., I went to the coronary lab and was given the cauterization. Although 40 percent of my heart was not working, the doctors were astonished that I had no blockage left and no need for surgery.

One week later, I was released. The doctor said that I could possibly recover some of the damaged heart over time, but I would still probably suffer 15 to 20 percent damage to the heart muscle.

Several weeks later, I returned to the hospital for a stress test and was eager to talk to the nurse who had been so reassuring. I scanned all the faces and met some of the nurses who had attended me that night. They firmly assured me that no such nurse had been with me that night in the room! I also learned that hospital policy would never have allowed any nurse to say such things to me, since my prognosis at that time was dire!

Fifteen months later, my heart doctor dismissed me and said that he was amazed that my heart muscle showed no damage. He said, "Whatever you've done has worked!" Since that time, I had unrelated, minor surgery at the hospital and had to inform them that I'd had a heart attack, which surprised them since my EKG showed no problem with my heart at all. They even asked me if I was sure.

What I *am* sure about is that the kindly nurse was my very own guardian angel!

❧ ❧ ❧

CHAPTER FIVE

Children Who Have Seen Apparitions of Their Deceased Loved Ones

The Grandfather I'd Never Known
by Luann Brown

When I was 16, on the night of December 20, at 2:10 A.M., the phone rang with the news that an ambulance had just been called for my grandmother, who was very ill. My dad met her at the hospital, and they admitted her to the intensive care unit, saying she'd had a heart attack. When he left, she was okay and able to talk to him. My grandmother had lived with us since I was five years old, and she and I were very close. We shared many special stories throughout these years, and she was more like a mother to me.

When my dad came home, he told us all the details about Grandma's condition and said she was resting comfortably. The next morning at 7:30 A.M., I was drying my hair in my bedroom in front of the mirror. My parents had gone to work already, and I saw a man standing in my doorway. He said, "Your grandmother has passed away." I turned around, but there was nobody there!

I was so scared that I called my father at work, who told me to call the police and that he would be right home. He worked about five minutes from our house, and the police were here when he got home. They searched our house and found nothing. After the police left, my father drove me to school. Nobody ever asked me if the man had said anything. After school, my parents were there to pick me up, which they'd never before done. We got home, and my father then told me that my grandmother had indeed passed away.

All I said was I that I already knew. He asked me how I knew, and then I told him what the man had said. Dad began to sob. To this day, he swears it must have been his father telling me. His dad had passed away when my father was just 14.

Ariel's Visit from Grandpa
by Mary Ellen

When my daughter, Ariel, was eight years old, I learned that she had many spiritual gifts. Ariel could see auras, she could hear her guides and angels, and she could tell you about the integrity and intention of people.

One night, Ariel called to me from her bedroom. In her sweet and gentle voice, she said that her grandfather was asleep in the extra bed in her room. Ariel's grandfather had died six years before. I was a little nervous about why he was in her room and if it "spooked" her.

So I asked Ariel why he was there, and she replied, "He has come to see how I have grown."

From that moment, I was at peace with her gifts. I knew that they were a gift from God that she was open to, and that these gifts would protect and guide her in life in a way I never could. When a mother knows that her child is guided by angels, it makes child rearing a joy and not a worry.

We Believe Her
by Tara Gibbs Kieninger

In April of 1998, my stepfather, Emile, passed away unexpectedly after routine hernia surgery. He was only in his early 50s when he died, so our grief was quite intense. Shortly after his death, my best friend, Michelle, and her husband, Rob, were talking about him. Michelle's daughter, Rebecca (who was only two at the time and had only met my stepfather shortly on a couple of occasions), was in the room. Michelle reminded her that Emile was now in heaven. Rebecca looked at her mom and said, "No, Mom, he's sitting right there," as she pointed to the chair next to her. Michelle asked her, "Where is he?" and Rebecca replied again, "He's sitting right there," as she pointed to the same spot. She was absolutely convinced that he was sitting next to her, and we believed her.

ᴡᴡᴡ

My Baby Talks to Heaven
by Elizabeth Marie Newsome

I am a mother of two very precious boys, Tyler, three and a half years; and Ryan, ten months. Recently my great-grandmother, Nana, passed away due to complications from Alzheimer's.

One night we were eating dinner, and Ryan started calling out, "Nana! Nana!" At first we just thought he was making a new sound, but he continued to say, "Nana! Nana!" So I asked him, "Where is Nana?" He just smiled real big, and I went back to eating. Again, he called her and again, I asked where she was. This time, Tyler said, "Nana's up in heaven; she's a star."

Later, we all went to take baths and get ready for bed. Ryan and I were in the tub, and he started calling our Nana again—only this time, he was looking up at the ceiling and holding his hands up to her. I was amazed, and it was an experience that I will cherish forever.

❦❦❦

I'll Be Here, Waiting for You
by Diane Lynn Willard Zarro

I was nine years old when my grandmother died of a massive heart attack. I had just found out about her death, and I locked myself in the bathroom so I could be alone. I had never known anyone who had died before and began wondering where she had gone, what really happened to her soul, and similar concerns. I had only been to church a few times as a child, but I had a deep belief in God and talked to Him through prayer every night. So in the bathroom alone, I began praying, asking for some kind of sign that my grandmother still existed, that she wasn't alone, or frightened in the dark, feeling pain.

Almost immediately, my grandmother appeared across the room, in a shimmering translucent cloud. It looked as though I were peering through an aquarium full of water. My simple grandmother, usually plain, looked so beautiful and happy. She was dressed in a pretty turquoise dress, and her hair was done up as if she were going out to a special event.

She spoke. She wasn't actually moving her mouth, but her voice was clearly projected into my mind. She said, "Hi, honey. I only have a little time, but I want to let you know that I'm okay. I'm here with my mother, my sister, and the rest of my family that has passed on." Tears welled up in my eyes, and I became afraid. Her image instantly started to blur, and she said, "I don't want to frighten you, so I'll go now."

I said aloud, "No, don't go. I'm sorry. I'm not afraid. Oh, God, please don't take her away yet. Please stay!" As my grandmother's image disappeared, she said, "I can't stay. I only have a couple more moments with you. I really shouldn't be here now. But I wanted to be sure you knew that I'm all right. I'm happy, and I have no more pain. I'll be here waiting for all of you when it's your time, many years from now." And she was gone.

This experience helped me to know that God has a direction for each of us. I'm not afraid of death for myself, and I know that when my other family members pass on, they *will* go on to a greater place.

It was a precious moment in my life, and I'll never forget it.

Don't Be Sad
by Bill Fletcher

We lost my youngest daughter, Emma, in February 1990, when her best friend called to her from across a road, and she ran out into the path of a car without looking. She was put on life support at the hospital, but it became obvious that she was not going to recover. Emma passed away in the hospital.

My eldest daughter, Elizabeth, was too grief-stricken to sleep in the room she had shared with her sister, so we moved her bed into our room. Two Sundays later, she said that she had seen Emma the previous evening and felt comfortable returning to her own bedroom.

When I asked what happened, Elizabeth replied that Emma had stood at the side of her bed and said, "Don't be sad, I'm all right now." I asked if it was a dream, and Elizabeth said she was sitting up in bed talking to her, so it couldn't have been.

Emma's friend, who had called her across the road, came to me excitedly a couple of days after and said that she, too, had seen Emma. Emma had said to her, "Don't be sad. It had to happen, and I'm all right now."

I Saw My Aunt, Even Though I Hadn't Met Her or Heard About Her!
by Mary Anne Luppino

When I was seven years old, I had a dream that a snake bit my ankle, and it actually hurt so much that I awoke and sat up suddenly. I saw a figure in the doorway of my room who looked exactly like my mother. I reached out for her, crying. When I did so, she slowly disappeared. In the next moment, my babysitter came in to see why I was crying. It turned out that my mother wasn't even home yet.

In later years, I realized that the spirit I saw was my mother's sister, Belle, who had died when she was 18. Belle and my mother looked almost exactly alike. Years later, a psychic who didn't know about my deceased aunt informed me that a woman named Belle was my guardian angel. She described Belle and told me what kind of dress she was wearing. When I told my mother the description, she started to cry, because that was her sister's favorite dress.

She Really Sees Him
by Joanne P. Hull

My little great-granddaughter, Faith Lene Cline, aged two and a half years, keeps telling her mom and grandma that "Chawie is here." Chawie is her uncle, Charles Arthur Fleming, who passed away last year at the age of 12. So last year, Faith would have been only one and a half years old, and I doubt that she really remembers him.

❊ ❊ ❊

CHAPTER SIX

Adults Who Have Seen Apparitions of Their Deceased Loved Ones

Thank You, Dad!
by Peggy Keating

My father died in 1973. Approximately two years later, he saved my life. I was driving late at night, very tired and sleepy. Foolishly, I was determined to keep going. I was drifting off to sleep, and suddenly there stood my father at the side of the road! He had a full body and was wearing the same kind of clothing he did when his body was alive—there was no mistaking him. When I looked in the rearview mirror, he was gone. Needless to say, I was wide awake for the rest of the trip. Thank you, Dad!

Watching Over Us
by Catherine Kilian

My father, William, passed away from a massive heart attack when I was 13. We had a tight father-daughter relationship and did almost everything together. His passing was very tough on me because not only did I lose my father, I lost my best friend.

Eight years later, I was seven months pregnant with my first child—who would have been my father's first grandchild. My husband and I had just finished the nursery, and completely exhausted, we had turned in early. In the early morning hours, I needed to use the bathroom, and when I opened the door, my father was standing right at the threshold of the nursery, looking in. He turned, saw me, and smiled. Scared, I slammed the door shut. After realizing what I had seen, I opened the door again, and he was still there, smiling. He walked into the nursery and disappeared.

I know he is watching over my daughter every minute, and I know in my heart that he loves her.

❦❦❦

A Mother's Eternal Love
by Kay Allenbaugh

I couldn't believe that I was entering a sweat lodge, a place of Native American ritual. I'm blonde, blue-eyed, and mostly German. At the time, I was 43, the mother of four grown boys, and working at a hospital, when my husband, Eric, and I took a vacation to the beach with a group of alternative healers.

When we were offered the opportunity to participate in the Indian ceremony, Eric didn't hesitate. He's like that—an "I'll try anything once" kind of guy when it comes to new adventures. Me—I need to be prodded along.

I was still resisting as the 12 of us sat cross-legged in a circle inside the tiny, five-foot-high tentlike structure made up of poles and branches. The Indian medicine woman began chanting and giving praise to the spirits. My heart raced. I watched fearfully as fiery rocks were piled in the center of our circle. Can rocks explode? Will we run out of air? Will I pass out?

Everything felt too tight. I tried desperately to control my wild breathing. It was so hot that, in sheer panic, I leaned forward, placing my face in the dirt to cool off.

An hour later, I stumbled out of the lodge. I was totally drained and exhausted. I collapsed, outstretched on the sand. Yes. That was it. I was safe and out in the fresh air. I expected no more. Then, just as I gazed up at the stars, my mother's image appeared before me. I was stunned. (My mother had died at 40 when I was just 15 years old.) Her smiling face took up the space of the full moon.

She began speaking to me in words that only I could hear. "Look at you!" she said. "You've done so much and come so far. You've had opportunities I never had." She was very pleased with me, and I could feel her love envelop me.

Heartrending occurrences flashed through my mind. I thought of important events that I hadn't been able to share with my mother, such as my anguish at the time of her death, finding my stoic twin brother outstretched across his bed sobbing and grieving six months later, my senior prom, my high school and college graduations, Mother's Day each year, my wedding day, my children, a painful divorce, a wonderful second marriage, and career changes. I also wanted to share my spiritual hunger, my tears and laughter, my love of movies, seeing mothers and daughters together, and much more. I thought that she had missed all of this. Now I knew that she had been there with me all my life.

She faded away after a few minutes, and I lay there feeling sheer joy and wonder, bathing in the warm afterglow. I can't explain it, yet I know it was real.

If I had chickened out of going to that sweat lodge, I would have missed one of the most memorable experiences of my life. I was given this sweet opportunity to heal, and to hear Mom say, "I love you, dear daughter."

Dad Always Encouraged Me
by Andrea

I was in my early 30s and trying to get into law school. Becoming a lawyer was a personal dream of mine, and my dad and I always talked about it. When I first tried to gain admission to law school after receiving my bachelor's degree, I didn't do too well on the entrance exams, so I gave up. My Dad wanted me to keep trying, but I didn't.

Soon after, though, my Dad died. He was only 48, and he just died too young. For Dad's sake, I decided to try applying to law school again. So I again took the LSAT entrance examination, and even though I studied hard, I still didn't do that well on the test. But I was determined to pass, so I applied to law school anyway, hoping that my good university grades would offset my poor showing on the law boards.

A few weeks after I applied for law school, a friend called to tell me that she got accepted to my hoped-for school! I was very happy for her, but very sad for myself. Since I hadn't heard anything, and my friend *had*, I naturally concluded that I hadn't been accepted into law school. I cried and just wanted to give up. Everything I had worked so hard for was again going out the window. I was so upset that I just shut myself away from everyone. I couldn't believe that this had happened to me again. I was devastated.

That night—I will never forget this—I was asleep, and my room lit up with a very bright light. It was so bright that the light woke me up. That's when I saw my dad in the center of the light. He told me that everything was going to be okay, and that I was going to be accepted by the law school. He said that I would definitely finish the law school program, and that my dreams of becoming a lawyer would come true.

I was so happy to see him! I wanted him to stay and talk to me, but he said he came just to tell me he was okay and was watching over me and things were going to turn out all right. I begged him not to go, to just stay and talk. He told me he had to go, and that his work with me was done, but that he would be with me always.

Two days later, I received the news that I had been accepted into law school! Just like Dad had promised, I graduated. Since then, I've passed the bars in two states and can practice law in both. My story may sound strange, but I know for a fact that my Dad was there, and I won't ever forget it.

❦❦❦

A Green Light from Grandpa
by Tammy Zienka

While I was in my freshman year attending Kent State University in 1987, my Grandpa Jim had a cardiac arrest while alone in his room at Veterans Hospital in Cleveland. When the staff found him several minutes later, they resuscitated him. Since he had gone for several minutes without air, they could only bring him back to a coma state in which he was unable to respond to any verbal or physical stimuli. The only thing that kept him alive was the respirator. After five days, there were still no signs of life in my grandfather, not even an attempt to breathe on his own. The doctors said that he was "clinically" dead.

At this point, we had a family meeting to discuss the idea of signing an order that would allow Grandpa Jim to be taken off of artificial life-support measures (called a DNR, or Do Not Resuscitate order). Everyone agreed, except for my uncle, who wanted to wait a few more days in the hopes that Grandpa Jim would awaken and be as he always was. After this meeting, I drove back to school. It was pretty late at night, and there was not a lot of traffic on the roads. During the drive, I was feeling angry with my uncle and grieving the loss of my grandpa, the person who had the greatest positive impact on my life.

I came to a stop sign and was the only car at this intersection. I looked to the right of me and noticed the front lawn of a house that was right there. I saw the spirit of a priest standing next to the bird bath on the front lawn. He had a small frame, was about 5'5" tall, and he was wearing an old traditional robe with a hat like a bishop's. He appeared to be performing a rite. He was making the sign of the cross with his hands. The more I looked at him, the brighter he got.

Then, on the other side of the bird bath, Grandpa Jim appeared. He stood tall and dignified, the way I always knew him. He wore a navy blue coat and white pants, just like he wore when he was in the Navy. His face was glowing, and he was at peace. I could feel him tell me that he wanted us to "let him go"—to sign the DNR order. I nodded to him, and he smiled at me. I turned to look at the traffic light and noticed that it was green.

When I looked back, my grandfather and the priest were gone. When I got back to my dorm room, I called my mother and told her what had happened. Until this point, I did not understand why I saw the priest. When I described him to my mother, she told me that Grandpa Jim had a friend who was a priest who had died ten years earlier. My description of him matched my mother's. That was confirmation to her and the rest of my family that what I saw was real.

At the next family meeting, I told everyone about my vision. I assured them that Grandpa Jim was at peace and that it was time for us to let him go. I also reassured them that he was and is still with us. Finally, my uncle agreed to the DNR order, and the document was signed. The following week, on Thanksgiving Day, Grandpa Jim's heart arrested, and he passed on. For many days after his death, I saw green auras around every light. Like the green traffic light that I saw immediately after my vision, the color green means "go," and maybe that was his way of saying, "Thank you for letting me go."

Sparkling with Joy
by Brooke Bennett

I experienced a most memorable visitation one morning, upon awakening. My mother, who had died several days before, appcarcd to mc. Hcr facc was glowing, almost sparkling. Shc had the most joyful smile on her face, and she wore a dress with a rainbow of sparkling colors. When my mother came to me, I was so very excited to see her. I felt so much joy coming from her that it was palpable. I was in awe of what I was seeing and feeling and called to her, "Mama, Mama!" Tears of joy came to my eyes. She did not speak, but she didn't need to. She communicated everything through the vision. It is one of my happiest memories of my mother.

❦❦❦

I'm Sorry That I Couldn't Wait
by Kelly B. Norman

In 1991, I was overseas on a six-month deployment as a U.S. Marine. My father was back home, dying of leukemia, and I knew that it wouldn't be long. At every port, I would go to the phone center and call my father to see how he was doing.

When I called my father from a Gulf country called Bahrain, I knew from the sound of his voice that he was very weak. I asked him how he was doing, and he said he was in a lot of pain and that he didn't know how much longer he would be able to hold on. I asked him to hold on until I was home so I could be with him before he died. He told me he would try to wait for me. I had three more months to go before my deployment was over.

Some of my friends and I were on a bus heading for the USO, when somehow we started talking about my father. I found it very strange, and knew that there was a reason why. I was just hoping that the reason wasn't the one I was thinking of. The next morning, about 0800, the company First Sergeant came into the building, and I knew instantly why he was there. "Sgt. Norman, you need to go to the company office and see the Commanding Officer."

I reported to the Commanding Officer, and as soon as he opened his mouth, I started to cry.

Within hours, I was on a plane out of the Gulf, heading back to Georgia for my father's funeral. Several days later, I saw a vision or I had a dream while I was lying in bed. I saw my father descending from the ceiling. He said, "Son, I came to tell you that I'm sorry I couldn't wait for you to return. I love you, son. Good-bye." And then he ascended back through the ceiling and was gone. I lay there wondering whether I was dreaming or if I actually just had a visit from my father. It seemed so real.

❦❦❦

Heavenly Matchmaker
by Melanie Wills

I grew up living with my grandmother for most of the time. I loved that woman more than life itself. Then she started having health problems. My grandmother was a very strong woman. You never saw her cry. Well, her pain was so severe that she cried constantly. I would sit and hold her hand and rub her back to help to relieve some of the pain.

I was doing this one evening in November of 1996, and she looked straight at me and cried, "Please God, take me, I can't stand this pain anymore." As much as I knew I would hurt if she left, I looked to God above and said, while holding her frail hand, "Please God, take her so she won't suffer anymore." I stayed with her awhile longer and then told her I needed to get home to prepare for work the next day. She said, "Okay, Baby, I love you.

Please take care of your mother for me." I knew that would be the last time I would see my grandmother alive. I hugged her and told her I loved her so much, and I thanked her for everything she had ever done for me. In the middle of the night, my grandmother passed on.

In April of 1998, I met the man of my dreams, and we soon married and had a beautiful baby girl.

In August of 1999, I was sitting in my bedroom, when the strangest feeling come over me. All of a sudden, standing before me, was my grandmother. She was so beautiful, and I could tell that she was pain free. There was a glow around her, and it was as if wind was blowing her gown. She said, "My baby, I love you." Then she started to walk away. I said, "Wait a little bit. Please don't go yet. I want you to meet Kevin, my husband, and to see our precious little girl." She turned to me and said, "Honey, I knew Kevin a long time before you did. This is why I passed on. Can you understand what Nanny is saying, sweetheart? I passed on so that I could find Kevin for you. I searched and searched, and he is the one I wanted my baby girl to be with. You have a precious little girl. I know that. I was there." She said, "I love you," and turned and walked away into a bright hallway. I started to say "I love you" back, but she was gone. I truly believe she is my angel.

❧❧❧

My Mother, the Angel
by Betsy Williams

Fifteen years ago, my mother was in the hospital dying of lung cancer. I knew that she was very scared of dying alone in the hospital, so even though she was in a coma, my husband and I stayed with her all day and night until she died. We just about lived at the hospital for the last three weeks of her life. On the day she died, before I left the hospital, I kissed her good-bye and said it was okay for her to leave.

Later that night as I was sleeping, I kept hearing my mother saying my name. I was asleep, and I remember waking up, but my eyes were still closed. I heard my mother say "Betsy" very clearly. I sat up, and at the foot of my four-poster bed was my mother. She looked youthful, as if she were 35 or 40 years of age. My mother was smiling at me, and wearing a long white flowing garment that sparkled in a way that I can't even describe. She looked so beautiful!

She was surrounded by the brightest light I have ever seen, and she said, "Betsy, I'm fine. Everything is okay. I love you. Don't worry about me." Then she was gone. I know it wasn't a dream; my mother was trying to show me she was okay, and I think she was thanking me for my love. Since then, I have had no doubt about God or the angels. I know they surround me always.

***

My Baby's Guardian Angel
by Janice

My grandfather from my dad's side passed away when I was 13, and I was so close to him. When I had my first baby at 21, he appeared to me, and I will never forget it! I had just fed my son and had laid him back in the bassinet next to my bed. All of a sudden, I felt cold, and there at the foot of my bed stood an image. I really couldn't make it out, and it scared me. I couldn't talk, move, or scream. This image starting moving toward the bassinet, and I couldn't do anything. Then it spoke, and I realized it was my grandfather.

He told me, "Don't be afraid. I just wanted to see my great-grandson." He leaned over the bassinet and touched my baby. Then he disappeared, and I have never felt his presence again. I immediately picked my baby up and called my mom. She reassured me that it was okay, because the same thing happened to her with *her* dad when my oldest sister was born. I *do* believe in angels, and I know that they surround me and my kids!

I Will Always Be with You
by L.D.D.

In 1981, my mother passed away, and I was very upset. She was only 47 years old, and her death was completely unexpected. I was 21 years old at the time of her death, and going through a divorce. My church had kicked me out because they said I had no grounds for divorce.

After my mom's funeral, I was at home, feeling very concerned that she was at peace and was reunited with my father, who had also passed away. No one else was home that day except for my daughter, who was in bed asleep. At that moment, I heard someone rattle the doorknob. I was going to the door when I saw my mother standing there in the clothes I had buried her in. I was shocked. She said, "I have come to let you know it is beautiful where I am. Don't worry any longer. I will always be with you."

Since then, she has talked to me and come to me at other times. My daughter has also seen her. We have been told by others that there is no such thing as life after death, or that it's evil to see and talk to a spirit . . . but we know what we have seen, felt, and heard, and we believe this to be very real.

A Warning from Above
by Anonymous

When my brother and sisters and I were all young children, my father went to Houston for his job, so my mother and four young children lived together in our home. My mother was sleeping when she woke up smelling a particular fragrance: her mother's perfume.

She opened her eyes to see the form of her mother, who was saying, "Wake up, turn on the porch light!" My mother said, "No, I'm tired," as she was half-asleep. But her mother was insistent and emphatic: "Get up now and turn on the light!" So my mother got up, turned on the lights around the house, and then went back to bed.

The next morning, my mother picked up the phone, only to discover that the phone line was dead. The telephone repairmen discovered that our phone lines had been cut, and they also found footprints under my bedroom window, so they went next door to call the police.

The repairmen said that the person who cut the lines really knew what he was doing, as the phone lines were underground. The police said that we were very lucky, because when phone lines are cut, the perp has a much more sinister plan than just robbery. Putting on the lights in the house must have scared him away. "Boy, were you lucky," the police said. However, my mother knew there was a lot more than luck involved, and she silently thanked her mom.

Beautiful in the Light
by Sally M. Basso

Luraine was a friend for 50 years, and she was stricken with cancer about three years ago. She told no one about her illness until a year ago. I sent her healing audiotapes and used hypnotherapy on her over the phone. She was not in the hospital, but she would receive treatment there every day. I would call her daily, but sometimes after a very difficult day, she couldn't call me back. Such a day occurred on a Saturday morning. But this time, the reason she didn't call me was because she had passed away.

That night, I was getting ready to go to sleep when I saw a figure in a purple shroud. Then the shroud fell off the figure's head and shoulders, and there in a beautiful light, I saw Luraine. She appeared youthful, as she did when she was about 30. She looked very beautiful and healthy. Luraine wore a beautiful white-velvet off-the-shoulders blouse, and she smiled with a very heavenly look. I went to sleep feeling very happy. The next day, I told her husband and daughter about the apparition, and they took joy in knowing that she was no longer suffering.

〰〰〰

When I Needed Him Most
by Kimberly Miller

About five years after my father died, I was going through a very stressful divorce. I was moving out on my own with two of my children, and I wasn't very confident. I started having horrible nightmares every night. One night, instead of a nightmare, I was awakened by a feeling of someone sitting on my bed. Thinking my youngest had come to sleep with me, I looked up. I was astounded to see the silhouette of my father sitting at the end of my bed. He didn't say anything; he just sat there. This continued nightly for about two or three months, and I never had a nightmare after that time. The appearances quit just about the time that things were starting to come together and I was becoming comfortable with myself. I realized that although my dad never said anything, he was there to comfort me when I needed him most.

CHAPTER SEVEN

Seeing Ascended Masters

Mother Mary Lifted Me Up
by Michelle Haynes

I was just about to finish college, and it seemed as if so many challenging things were going on in my life. I was having a difficult time letting go of college life, and was also experiencing a deep depression. If that weren't enough, many important people in my life were moving away.

The most significant loss I experienced was my therapist moving on. I was seeing her at a university counseling center where brief therapy was the norm because most of the counselors were interns in training. I had the rare opportunity to work with her for two years on and off; however, termination was inevitable.

With all of the changes and losses, I was depressed to the point of considering suicide. To help relieve my feelings of despair, I decided to go on a silent retreat. I go away every so often to be by myself as a means of regrouping, and to escape the hustle and bustle of daily life. I usually stay at a retreat center where retiring nuns live. Going to the retreat center has always given me a sense of solace. To this day, I look forward to going away for a couple of days where I don't speak to anyone. I just spend time being with myself and talking to God. It gives me great comfort.

While I was on this particular retreat, I felt peaceful even though I was experiencing depression. On the second night of my stay, something happened that in many ways was indescribable. I had just finished journaling and reading books on spirituality and had fallen asleep with the lights still on.

All of a sudden, the lights seemed to dim. I began to hear a humming sound like a thousand bees buzzing. Then I began to feel myself leaving my body. Initially, I was terrified of the experience, but then started saying to myself in my mind, "Let go, let God." As I continued to repeat this mantra, I felt myself lift out of my physical body until I was floating in the room.

I then noticed a white flowing entity enter the room. At first, I could not make out the entity, but then I realized that it was Mother Mary. She took my hand and led me outside of the retreat center. Then, somehow we were flying in the air. I remember seeing the night lights all around me. It was an incredible sight. As we were flying, she took me to a place where I began communicating with three incredible bright lights.

To this day, I have no idea what the three entities spoke to me about. I just remember being suspended in midair over what appeared to be California, of all places! The three entities were formed in a triangle. As each light spoke to me, the entity would become brighter while the other entities lessened in intensity. Whatever they said to me changed my life. I then returned with Mother Mary back to my room at the retreat center and went gently back into my body. I could hear a warm buzzing and tingling sensation as I did so.

I immediately rose from my bed and knew that this experience was more than just a dream. My depression broke, and things in my life started to turn around for the better. I will never forget this experience as long as I live.

A Saint by My Mother's Side
by Virginia E. Perry

My mother was hospitalized with leukemia, and after repeated, fruitless blood transfusions, the doctors and my sister finally decided it was her time to join Papa in heaven. Mama was afraid to die, for she thought the devil was waiting to grab her. By phone, I tried to reassure Mom that only friendly faces and Papa would be on hand to greet her on the other side.

I was unemployed, living in California at the time. Needless to say, I was greatly saddened that I didn't have the plane fare to be with her. I meditated on the situation, finally seeking help from my dearest guide, St. Therese. She has even appeared to me once or twice while I've helped ailing friends.

Boldly, I asked St. Therese to go to Mom since I couldn't be there. Months after Mom's death, I was talking with my sister, Ramona. She volunteered the information that a sweet little nun had kept constant vigil by Mom's side. When I asked her, Ramona told me the color of her habit, and her name was Sister Therese! Thank you, God, and dear Sister Therese. You have never failed to answer my prayers!

❦❦❦

He Was Right
by Linda A. Harlow

My husband and I were not happy together. One particular day was extremely sad for me, complete with the hand-wringing, tears, pleading to God for help, and "poor me" thoughts. That night, when I was lying in bed next to my snoring husband, feeling extremely unloved and lonely, a very odd thing happened. I saw a huge glowing-white Jesus-type fellow standing at the foot of the bed. His arms were stretched out, his head was going through the ceiling, and his feet were going through the foot of the bed. His whole body was very white and glowing, but I couldn't actually see his feet. He wore a white robe-type outfit. He also said the words, "You're both going to be all right."

That visit has sustained and strengthened me for almost another 30 years. We divorced, and although there have been very difficult as well as extremely rewarding times since then, I

have absolutely no doubt that I was "visited"—if not by Jesus himself, then by an angel. It doesn't really make much difference who was standing there that night; I just know he was right. Both my ex-husband and I are fine now.

I Saw Jesus
by Gwendolyn Wiles

About four years ago, I was driving in my neighborhood, just cruising alone. I am a sky watcher: I love to look at the stars, moon, and clouds. On that particular day, I was at a traffic light up the street from my house. I looked up, and there in the sky I saw Jesus Christ. I swear that I am not making this up.

He was standing there in the sky with a long white robe on, no shoes, brown shoulder-length hair, with his arms outstretched before him. And I looked and blinked and looked again, and he was still there, standing with outstretched hands, looking straight forward. The light changed, and I moved on. I never told too many people because I figured they wouldn't believe me. But I know that on that day I saw Jesus.

Jesus Healed Me
by Debbie Graham Hoskin

I had an experience about 20 years ago when I was on the road, singing professionally seven nights a week across the country for the Sheraton Hotel chain. Because of the grueling schedule and lack of rest, I began having trouble with my voice. My voice was usually hoarse in the morning, but after resting it all day, my voice would return each evening. After several months of this schedule, it became increasingly difficult to recover my voice at night.

One morning, I woke up and my voice was worse than ever. I was very upset at the thought of letting the band members down, not to mention the audience. I decided to pray, because I didn't know what else to do. I closed my curtains, put a "Do Not Disturb" sign on my door, and took the phone off the hook. I was on my knees on the floor. I said very firmly, "God, you must fix my voice. I know you are there, and I know that you hear me. I beg you to heal my voice. I will not leave this floor until you heal my voice. I know that you hear me. I believe you can heal me." I prayed intensely for about three hours.

I started to feel a presence in the room, as if someone had just walked through the door. I looked over at the door and saw the face of Jesus. I became paralyzed with fear. He took the fear away from me and told me telepathically, "I am love and kindness." He and his message were so strong that it overcame me. He approached me. I felt a hand brushing across my throat, and I felt intense heat in that area. Then I felt the presence leave. I broke out into a sweat. I was healed, and I thanked God.

The experience changed me as a person and also changed the way I perceived life. No matter what problems I experienced, I always knew that God was my friend. It took me ten years to tell anyone about that incident. I was certain that no one would believe me. I still sing and perform; however, I became driven to fulfill a higher purpose on this earth. I now work with victims of abuse.

An Indescribable Love
by Janine Cooper

I was living in Santa Monica in a single-unit guest house. During the month of June, it was often foggy, so my morning ritual was to look out the window upon awakening to see if bright light was shining in.

On this particular early morning, I had a very vivid and life-changing dream. Or was it a dream? In the "dream," I sat up in bed and looked at the window. There on the rice blind was the shroud of Jesus—just his face, about three to four feet in size. I said to myself, "Hey, that's Jesus!" And just as I said that, his face came in very clear, and a bolt of white light came out of it and right at me. The light had a paralyzing effect on me! I sat in bed and looked at my hands, and they were frozen stiff. I remember that my jaw was clenched, too. It was almost as if I'd had a seizure, but the feeling was one of total bliss.

I was not afraid at all. In fact, I have never felt more loved in my life. It was as though the light was made of love. As the feeling of being paralyzed eased up and the light faded away, I heard a voice say, "This is just a small sample of the power of God's love." The light withdrew, and the vision of Jesus faded away.

I awoke, sat up in bed, and sobbed for about a half hour! It was as though I had received a major healing, a gift of what is available to us anytime we ask for it. And it is so powerful! It was by far the most amazing and meaningful experience I've had in this lifetime.

The Healing Trio
by Anonymous

I saw an apparition of Archangel Raphael, Jesus, and what I believe to be my spirit guide—an old wise man from Tibet. This happened last year when my husband was in ill health.

My husband had a very high fever and a cough that was deep and full of congestion. One night was especially bad. I prayed and asked for God and the angels to assist in the healing of my husband. All of a sudden, Raphael, Jesus, and a spirit guide appeared in the right corner of my bedroom. Bright white lights surrounded the trio. I received instructions from the figures to place my hands on my husband's back (the lung area) and other parts of his body so that the healing would occur. I know that one of the images was Raphael for sure, because I asked for him specifically, knowing all about his mission of healing from reading Doreen Virtue's books.

I know that the other image was Jesus. I am not a fan of Jesus and was disappointed that he was there. Basically, I believe that he lived; I just don't believe that he was the son of God. I asked the universe why Jesus was with Raphael and the Tibetan man. I was angry that Jesus was there. The answer came quickly. I was told that he had healed many people and that he had come as a result of my request for healing. Needless to say, my husband recovered directly after this sighting. Additionally, I have been more at peace about Jesus since then—I have no more anger.

We've Got Work to Do
by Steve Jordan

This experience occurred during Easter week while I was living in Portland, Oregon. I had just watched a television program about Jesus being crucified. In the middle of that same night, I woke up with fear, without knowing why I was feeling that way. Then, a feeling went through me, and it calmed me down. I lay on my back looking directly up at the ceiling. My eyes were wide open; however, I was very quiet.

Additional calmness started to settle into my body. I was opening up to whatever was coming my way. I started to realize that God was there, and I could strongly feel His presence. Of course, I could not see Him, but I could feel His love and compassion for me. Then Jesus started to appear on the right side of me.

I could see Jesus crystal-clear. His hair was brown, and he had a small beard. The length of his hair was medium to short. He wore a white robe, with a blue cloth across his chest that extended down to his feet. He was more than seven feet tall and had the most loving and compassionate expression on his face. I felt his love as strong as I did that of God's. But God was much stronger, and there was much more determination in His being.

Jesus's face was free of winkles. He had crystal-blue eyes. There was a dim light around him, but a very powerful light in shades of white, mixed with yellow. I felt that he did not want to blind me with too bright of a light around him, and that he had dimmed its brightness for my benefit. Every time Christ moved, the light would follow him as he floated.

Jesus finally spoke to me. "Come and follow me. We have work to do!" At the time, I was a deacon at the church I attended. After this experience, I helped start a church in Portland, Oregon, for our denomination, The Universal Fellowship of Metropolitan Community Churches. Let me tell you, this was the most beautiful experience I've ever had!

An Inner Operation
by Cheryl Cash

I went to India to see the avatar, Sathya Sai Baba. One night we left the door of our temporary residence open because of the heat. I felt Baba come into the room and bless my hands and my feet. I was thrilled, thinking, *Baba's here, and he is blessing me all over. I am blissful!*

Then I awoke to welts on my feet and hands, realizing that what I had felt were mosquitos. I was irritated with myself for my foolish thoughts, saying within, *Oh, it's not Baba. It's the mosquitos.* I then saw an image of Baba walking over to my bed. He shook his finger in my face and said, "No, Cheryl, I am in everything, including the mosquitos. I am always with you!"

Within a few weeks of returning home to Arizona, I had a vivid dream of Baba. My husband, Jim, is a very aesthetic person, meaning that he focuses on how people and things look. Jim didn't like the shape of my nose. It really bothered him, and he thought that if we were to marry, perhaps sometime I would get it surgically fixed. As an adolescent, I hadn't liked the shape of my nose, either. Jim's comments recharged my teenage angst about my physical appearance, and I became very self-conscious about my fat, ball-tipped nose.

I wondered what God thought of me for going along with this. I thought about Paramahansa Yogananda, and mostly, I wondered what Sai Baba thought. Was I a shallow person to get my nose fixed, to worry about keeping someone I loved by having surgery? Why was I giving this power over to someone else?

Well, in my dream, Baba came to me. He cocked his head from side to side, looking into my eyes with childlike play. Then he asked, "So, you do not like your nose?" and I shook my head. He then said, "I'll fix it. Follow me!" He went off into a large, bright orange tent, holding a needle in his right hand, up in the air. I followed him, thinking, *Oh, Baba's going to operate on my nose in my sleep—just like I read about!* But as I followed him into the tent, everything disappeared, and I woke up.

So I went to the bathroom to check my nose, fully believing that Baba had changed its appearance, but he hadn't. My nose still looked the same.

However, sometime later, Jim and I were married. When I mentioned looking for a good doctor to fix my nose, Jim had not only changed his mind, but he said that he couldn't understand why my nose had ever bothered him in the first place.

Mary Moved
by Anonymous

When I was five years old, I was in church with several other children, receiving instructions from our teacher. We sat in our pews, silently listening. I then saw something move out of the corner of my eye. I watched as the statue of Mother Mary, at the front of the stage, moved her hands toward me and the other children.

I didn't mention this to anyone, until I later found out that three other children in my class had seen the same thing, and they had reported their vision to their parents.

The Deepest Feeling of Safety
by Janie Daily

My mom died when I was seven and a half years old. She was a wonderful woman, who taught me more in those few years than most mothers can teach in a lifetime. After she died, my brothers and I were left to be raised by my grandmother. She didn't like girls and blatantly told me so. My life was hell, and often I thought of committing suicide.

There were times when I would hear a male voice saying my name. My grandmother frightened me so badly by telling me that it was Satan. Maybe that is what she was taught, who knows? Anyway, one night, I was so sad and was crying, missing my mom and just wanting to join her in death. At that moment at the bottom of my bed, I saw a bright white light. I looked harder, and in disbelief, I could make out the apparition of a man.

He spoke to me and told me that everything would be okay. I must tell you that at that

moment, I felt safer than I had ever felt. Today, at 38, I still can feel that secure, safe feeling. I knew it was Jesus.

❦❦❦

Beautiful Little Light
by Karen Noe

A few years ago, I had quite an enlightening experience. I was sitting on my bed when a beautiful light came toward me. At first I was frightened, but then an incredible peace came over me. The light emanated a voice! It spoke to me, saying, "Luce, lucina. Bella luce, lucina." I later learned that in Italian this means, "Light, little light. Beautiful little light." Since then, I have realized that it was St. Francis who came to comfort me at the time.

In my heart, I know that he has been with me ever since! He is definitely working with me in promoting peace in this world, and love for all of God's kingdom, which of course includes animals and plants. Birds and butterflies in particular have been ever-present for me. When I am driving my children across town, which is only five minutes away, birds and butterflies go right in front of my car and stay there, flapping their wings. I know it is common for birds to be flying around, but not right in front of someone's car.

On one ride across town, my youngest son counted nine birds that flew in front of my car, either right by my windshield or at ground level. One such bird made me slow down, thank goodness, because I was going much too fast. After I did so, I noticed a policeman at the end of the block. I giggled and thanked the bird silently for preventing me from getting a ticket.

)€)€)€

CHAPTER EIGHT

Dreams of Deceased Loved Ones

The Light and the Rose
by Cheryl Anne

In February of 1991, my mother-in-law passed away after a long battle with chronic obstructive pulmonary disease. She died a slow and painful death, and it was a very difficult time. My first-born son, her first grandchild, was only four months old at the time of her passing. I believe that her desire to see him kept her alive those last few months.

About a week after she died, I had a "dream" where I was somehow transported to the sanctuary of the church where my mother-in-law's memorial service had been held. For a short time, maybe a minute, I was alone. Then she appeared. She was so beautiful. She looked like herself, full-figured and round-faced, but glowing. I had never seen her looking so healthy and vibrant.

She greeted me in her jovial way and said, "Don't worry, I'm okay. I'm not sick anymore, it's so wonderful!" She was wearing a long, flowing, flowered gown. She said that she was wearing that gown because God had placed her in a garden, and that it was more beautiful there than anyone could imagine. I could actually smell the flowers as she described them. I felt total peace.

The next thing I remember, I was awakened by my husband. We both sat straight up in bed in complete shock. The hallway outside our bedroom was filled with a magnificent light. There were no lights on in the house, and it was well past midnight. Just as the light faded away, a rose that we had saved from the memorial service spun in its vase. I was so glad we had both witnessed this, or I would probably think I was crazy!

I Am Happy
by Pamela Wolfe

My father made his transition in 1989, following years of coping with diabetes, blindness, and two lower leg amputations. Despite these difficulties, he was not bitter. Instead, his life was a testimony to many people, and taught us that we can overcome with God's help. When he first went blind, he thought about committing suicide one day when he was alone. As he was standing in the living room with a gun, he felt a hand on his head. This hand pushed him to his knees, and his head landed on the Bible on the coffee table. From that day on, he surrendered to God and regained his will to live. We learned after he died that every Christmas season he gave someone in need a Bible.

I believe he came to me in a very vivid "dream" to show me that he is now completely healthy and happy. I dreamed that I was driving in my car and came to a huge brick building, parked my car, and went inside. I passed through the lobby and down a long hallway. I came to a room where the door was partially open. When I entered, there stood my father. Although he was about 57 years old when he died, he now looked around 30. He was smiling, and lots of white light was beaming out of him! I can't recall the entire conversation, but I do remember remarking that he looked very happy. He replied, "I *am* happy!"

Until We Can All Be Together Again
by Debbie Eyler

I never really had faith in angels until May of 1999. I was skeptical after losing my father when I was eight, and my uncle and all my grandparents soon after. Then on April 28, 1998, my sister (and best friend) died at the age of 38. This was the final straw, and I lost all faith and hope that life was good.

If that wasn't enough, on May 30, 1999, I received a call that an ambulance was transporting my mother to the hospital. We thought she'd had a stroke. On my way to the hospital, I closed my eyes and had a vision of my mother speaking to Phil, my late sister's husband. I could see her plain as day saying, "Phil, don't worry, I am here with Aileen (my sister), and it's all okay." The vision left me no doubt that my mother was already gone.

I believe it was her way of letting me know that she and my sister were together and doing well. It has renewed my faith a little, and it gives me some comfort to know that even though I am physically alone, they are all here with me. I know that they are pushing me forward until we can all be together again. I'm no longer afraid of dying.

I think that this faith has made me more open to hearing my angels. On December 26, 1999, a dear friend named Aaron passed away. He was only 24. We used to all get together and let our sons play together. His son, Luke, is 19 months, and mine is 18 months. The day he died, before I knew he was gone, I had a vision of him telling me to call his son's mother to tell her I would help her watch Luke whenever she needed someone. I believe it was Aaron's way of trying to look out for his son, whom he loved more than life itself.

Never Truly Lost
by Chuck Pekala

On June 1, 1998, my father passed on suddenly. My father and I were very close in our own way. Dad was born in the 1920s, and his family was not the most openly loving group of people. I had not embraced him since I was a child, and I had not kissed him since he came out of quadruple bypass surgery six years earlier. Still, we were close in a way that was comfortable for Dad, if not 100 percent fulfilling for me. And, we were both well aware of how much we loved each other.

I try very hard not to overlook special days for special people in my life, and Father's Day 1998 was no exception. I had purchased cards for Dad weeks before his passing. So, when the time came for his viewing, I felt it was very important to place his cards in his hands, and so I did.

In the cards, I wrote very personal notes to my father that I have not shared with a soul, but I needed to tell him some things one last time. I had to tell him that I loved him very much. I thanked him for being the best father he knew how to be, and I thanked him for never making me doubt his love. I told him I was glad he got to spend some retirement years with Mom, something I had prayed to God for all my life. And, I told Dad that even though I was now a man, I would still always be his one and only little boy. I knew that Dad was proud of me, and we had no unresolved issues. I closed the card by telling Dad that I would be thinking of him on Father's Day, and that I would take peace in knowing that he was with God.

Two weeks later, the Saturday before Father's Day arrived. That night, I went to bed with thoughts of my father. I had a wonderful dream in which my father walked in the room and stood silently. He looked at me and at first seemed somewhat confused, and then he slowly began to smile.

I asked, "Dad, are you okay? What do you want to tell me?"

Dad smiled and looked into my eyes. He replied, "I want you to know I am okay, Chuck. Do not worry. It is beautiful here, and I have never been happier." (Dad did not have an easy life.)

I woke up with an overwhelming sense of peace and security. My father was in God's care. The world was right again.

Another month passed, and my mother had a dream about my father. In her dream, he stood before her holding the hand of a small blond boy. My mother said, "I love you very much, and I miss you, honey." Dad smiled back and said, "I know." My mother looked at him again and said, "I am a bit confused. Who is that small boy with you?" My father replied, "I don't know, dear, but he was lost and told me he did not want to be alone, so I took his hand to keep him company."

The dream ended. My father loved children. I found this dream to be so typical of him, and I often wonder who that child was. I pray for them both. I hope that whoever lost that boy has had their own dream and knows he is well.

Perhaps reading my words will in some way comfort someone else who has lost a loved one. Actually, I don't care for the word *lost*, in this sense, since I believe that my father is still very much with me.

❦❦❦

We Both Talked to Dad
by Laura H.

Fifteen years ago when I was pregnant with my son, my grandmother was dying. I really wanted to go see her because she was my only link to my dad, who had died when I was 12. The doctors kept telling me I couldn't travel because I was at risk of losing the baby.

My husband and I kept arguing over it, and I still wanted to go. Well, I started spotting, and the doctor put me on total bed rest.

That night, I had a dream that I was sitting at a kitchen table with my dad. He was talking to me on the telephone, and I could hear him. He told me that it had been his time to die, that he was okay, that he loved me, and that it was time to get on with my life and think of my children and husband. It was so real. Then we walked down a dark tunnel, and at the end of the tunnel, he walked off into a bright light.

I woke up crying, but so much at peace. I called my mom to tell her the dream, and she started crying, too. She told me that my little sister had just called her and told her she had a dream about my dad, and when it was over, they, too, walked down a dark tunnel.

***

Reassurance from Grandma
by Tytti Vanhala

I live in the Netherlands, and when my grandma died, I felt very guilty that I never went to see her in the hospital. I just didn't want to go. Perhaps I wanted to remember her as she was before, and not as the shadow of her former self that she had become when she got sick.

Grandpa had died six months earlier, and we all thought that Grandma lost her reason for living when he passed on. I'd had some bad dreams after Grandpa's death. After Grandma died, I was a bit nervous and scared because I could feel the presence of both of them, as could my dad and two of my aunts. Their presence exacerbated my feelings of guilt about not visiting my grandma, and I wondered if she was angry with me.

One night, she visited me in a dream. I was bicycling with my boyfriend, and I could see my grandparents cycling toward us. They turned in front of us. I could see Grandpa, appearing quiet and grim, just as he was quite often when he was alive. Grandma cycled past me, almost unnoticed.

Soon I was cycling behind her, and I pleaded, "Grandma, please don't haunt me." She turned to face me. I noticed that her appearance hadn't changed from how she'd looked when she was living. Grandma smiled as she replied, "Why should I haunt you?" At that point, I woke up with a smile on my face and a warm feeling. The dream had been very real, and I realized that this was her way of letting me know that everything was okay, and she wasn't upset with me for not visiting her in the hospital. Maybe if she would have actually appeared to me, it would have been too much for me at that stage. I told my dad about my dream, and only then did he tell me that he saw her constantly. After that dream, she visited me now and then in other dreams.

Grandma's Red Rose
Susan E. Watters

It was 1972, the year I graduated from high school. My maternal grandmother had been ill for some time. She lived in another state and had wanted to see me for quite a while. We didn't have much money, and not even my mother could go that distance to see her. My aunt, who lived with her and took care of her, said she asked to see me all the time. My mother worked two jobs and was working her night job when I came home one night with Butch, my boyfriend at the time.

We were sitting on the couch, and the strangest feeling came over me. I told him that my grandmother had just died. He laughed and told me I was crazy. Just then, the phone rang. I told Butch I didn't want to answer the phone because I knew it was my uncle saying that my grandmother was gone. Again, Butch just laughed. I answered the phone, and it was, in fact, my uncle telling me that she had passed over just about the time I had said something to Butch. I called my mom at her job, and she came home. Mom went to her funeral out of state, but when she came back, she never said anything at all about the funeral.

The night after Mom came home, I dreamed that my grandmother was walking through my bedroom door. My first thought was, *How can this be? She's dead.* She continued to walk toward me, and I was afraid. I thought that I shouldn't be afraid because it was just Grandma. But then I would think, *She's dead!*

She looked younger than I had ever seen her, wearing a navy blue dress with big white polka dots, and she was smiling. I sat up on the edge of my bed, and she sat beside me. It was if we were talking, but through our minds, not our mouths. She knew I was scared and was telling me that it was okay. Grandma had a red rose in her hand that she wanted to give me, and I was afraid to take it. Again, she told me (with her mind, it seemed) that it was okay. I took the rose, she smiled, and I woke up. Or was I asleep, really? I don't think so. I believe that she visited me because she had wanted to see me. I woke up screaming, and my Mom came in my room.

I told her about the dream, and she said I was weird and walked out crying. Then she came back into my room and told me that Grandma had indeed looked a lot younger, was indeed buried in that very dress, and that she (my mom) had placed a red rose in her hands before they closed the casket. Yes, I believe in the spirit world that is beyond "life." No doubt about that.

In a Better Place
by Kim Carroll

My grandfather passed away several years ago in the hospital where I worked. When I heard a code blue while I was at work one day, I instantly knew in my heart that this meant that my grandpa had died. For weeks afterward, I felt sad that I was not with him at the moment he passed.

One night, I saw his reflection in a picture in my bedroom. He smiled, waved, and told me that everything was okay. A week later, I had a dream that I couldn't find my pet bird. In the dream, I was running down a staircase, and my grandfather met me on the stairs and told me everything was okay and safe and not to worry.

I loved my grandfather very much, and he had always told my family not to worry about him because he was prepared to die and that he would be in a better place. I feel he was reassuring me that he was in heaven and not to be afraid of death.

❦❦❦

(*Author's Note:* Sometimes, we don't actually *see* our deceased loved ones in dreams, but we know that they are responsible for prophetic ones.)

Saved by the Dream
by April Zeigler

About 16 years ago, I was living in Phoenix, Arizona. I shared an apartment with my one-year-old son. My husband and I were both in the Air Force. He was stationed in Korea at the time. I was a young mother going it alone, since my husband was away.

My apartment complex was a typical two-story building, with the front doors of the apartments facing a center courtyard and a pool. My apartment was on the second floor, the last one on the end, next to a stairwell, which was very overgrown with trees and plants.

As a young person, I had the tendency to be careless. I often left my apartment door unlocked, even forgetting to lock it when I went to bed at night. It was Friday night, and I had gone to bed, completely exhausted from working and taking care of my son, Heath.

That night I had a very strange dream. It wasn't the type of disjointed, crazy image that sometimes appear in one's mind, but more like a movie. In my dream, I was sitting in my living room. My couch faced the wall where the front door was, and off to the right was the television. In the dream, I vividly remember looking up at the clock on the wall over the TV, noticing that it was 1 A.M. I remember how the lighting was, almost a soft yellow light in the room. My son was sound asleep in his crib in the back room. Suddenly, my door flew open! I jumped up to get away, but a stranger came at me and fired a shot, which struck me in the stomach. I fell to the floor.

I could hear him head toward my son's room. Banging around, he woke up my son, who started to cry. Again, I heard another shot, and my son was no longer crying. I managed to almost get to my feet to help my son. Before I was completely standing, the stranger returned to the living room, placed the gun to my head, and fired.

I woke up from that dream, terrified. I couldn't believe what I had just seen! Eventually, I fell back to sleep. The next day, having put this dream out of my thoughts, my son and I continued about with our typical Saturday routine. Later that evening, I put my son to bed and just took it easy. Later on, I was sitting on the couch, in a sort of cross-legged position watching television. There was one soft light on. I remember feeling as if I had been here before: the lighting, the way I was sitting—it seemed so familiar, yet I couldn't place it. At that instant, I looked up at the clock, and it was almost 1 A.M., perhaps a minute till, just like in the previous night's dream.

Unconsciously, I must have remembered my dream, because I got up and walked over to the door and pressed the button in the middle of the doorknob to lock it. I hadn't even made a complete turn to walk back to the couch when the doorknob turned, as if someone were trying to open it. I immediately put the chain on the door and peeked out through the peephole. It appeared that my outside light was out. All I could see was a man pressed firmly against the door, as if he were trying to push the door open with his body.

I called out to him and asked him, "What do you want?" He replied, "I'm checking to see if you got the paper." I said, "I don't get the paper." He said, "Yeah, I know. My son delivers newspapers, and I need to check to see if you got yours. Can I come in?" I stepped back to think for a moment, then I remembered my husband's large rifle. I told the man, "Yeah, just a minute." I went to the closet, got the gun, which is a bolt-action rifle, placed the barrel of the gun to the door, pulled the bolt back (which is incredibly loud!), and said, "All right, you can come in now!" I heard the man's loud footsteps running down the second-floor walkway.

I didn't dare open my door. I called the police, and they came to my apartment. I was so scared that I almost didn't let them in until I looked out through my curtains and was positive a police officer was there. When I came out and explained to the policeman what had happened, he looked at me like I had just won the lottery. He said, "Ma'am, you don't know how lucky you are." He then explained that a man had been entering apartments of women who lived alone, raping them, robbing them, and killing them. What I had described as his method of trying to enter my apartment was the same one that another survivor described. She had been shot and left to die.

I was suddenly overcome with the realization that in my dream the night before, I had witnessed what was going to happen to me—except now, only an instant before I did something different from the dream, I got up and locked the door. I told the policeman this, and he said, "You must have one very good guardian angel!"

I believe that my deceased mother was responsible for coming into my dream and giving me this very clear warning.

❦❦❦

All Is Forgiven
by Jacki Whitford

My father passed away in January of 1981 at the age of 56 from alcohol abuse. We stayed with him that weekend, but on the day of his death, he told us all to go to work. It was a Monday, and he didn't want us to miss work on his account. I called frequently that day, up until about 8 P.M. that night. He passed away at 10 P.M. I was devastated that I did not have a chance to say goodbye and say a final "I love you."

Ten years later, I dreamed that I was standing on the street of my childhood home, next to the mailbox. I turned and looked through the night mist, waiting to see who was coming toward me. It was my father, looking like a healthy 30-something.

He said nothing, but just pulled me into his arms and held me. I felt an intense rush of bliss. Every fight we ever had, every negative thought and emotion, every trauma that had ever occurred between us—disintegrated into pure love. I heard someone sobbing, and realized I had awoken with a start. I felt as if I had been shoved back into my body. I no longer had issues with my father; I had a sense of closure. I also had a sense of what it's like in heaven: pure bliss, pure love, pure rapture.

❦❦❦

Messages Come to Those Who Are Open
by Judith Mitchell

My six-year-old daughter, Erin, came to me one morning and said, "I dreamed of Gramma last night." Sadness went through me. Her grandmother—my mother—had passed away suddenly and unexpectedly three months earlier. I admit that none of us grown-ups in the family were doing too well with our grief. I had hoped to dream about her myself, just to see her or hear her voice again.

I asked Erin what the dream was about. She told me that, in the dream, she was jumping on a trampoline at a friend's house when my mother appeared to her. She was light and so bright that you could barely look directly at her. She also had angel wings and a red halo. There were beams of light coming from her and surrounding her. She said, "Hello, Erin! How are you? I am doing fine. Why is everyone acting so silly about me being gone?"

Erin called out to her friends and their mother to come see her gramma, but when they came outside to the trampoline, they couldn't see her. Only Erin could. Erin asked, "Why can no one else see you? Why do you come to me and not the others?" Her grandmother answered, "Because you are the only one who is strong enough to see me right now; it is still too painful for them." And then she disappeared.

My daughter had three dreams like this one where her grandmother gave her messages. She was right—we were all too upset. Could we have withstood a message from her so soon after her death? Probably not. That was six years ago, and since then, we have had many visits, dreams, and forms of assistance from my mother. But my six-year-old was strong enough to see, listen, and believe when we adults were still too closed off with grief. My mother passed the message to Erin so that we would know that she is always there for us. We are all so grateful for this experience.

❦❦❦

A Load Was Lifted from My Shoulders
by Theresa Touchette

My mom passed away a year ago after a lengthy battle with breast cancer. She was only 52 years old. About six months after she died, my mother was on my mind a lot, and I wondered if she was okay.

Soon after, I dreamed that my mom was laying in bed in a beautiful white robe. She was in this plain, but very nice room. I was watching her sleep when she sat up in bed all of a sudden. My mom looked so pretty, with her hair and makeup done the way she had always worn it. She said to me, "I am fine. Tell everybody I am fine." When I woke up the next morning, I could remember every detail about her and the room. I felt as if a load had been lifted off my shoulders, because I now truly believe that she is doing okay. Every time I tell this story, it gives me goose bumps.

❦❦❦

Warm, Loving Energy
by Laura Riffel

I had been very close to a lady for quite some time. One day my daughter was babysitting her children and had some problems with one of her sons. I happened to be next door, so I stopped by to say hello. While I was there, I talked to the boy who was misbehaving. Later, when my friend heard that I'd talked to her son about his behavior, she became very angry. She thought my daughter had specifically called me to come talk to him. My friend then yelled at my daughter, which led to my friend and me having an argument. After that, we stopped talking to one another.

Then about a month ago, my friend died at the age of 29, very suddenly. I felt horrible about our unresolved fight. I fretted about it frequently. About two weeks after she passed on, I had a very vivid dream "encounter" with my friend.

In the dream, we were talking face-to-face in a very sunny and beautiful place. We talked about our fight and agreed that it was silly, and that we both were just protecting our children. She said it didn't matter, that everything was beautiful, and that I should forget about it, as she was not upset and I shouldn't be. Then she giggled, and I felt fluttering wings all over my back and saw a brilliant light.

At that moment, I woke up and was burning up with heat. My husband woke up at the exact moment and was also burning up with heat. We checked the thermostat, and it was turned down. I feel that the heat came from the extreme energy of my angelic visit. I truly believe that my friend visited me to ease my suffering over our fight.

※※※

She Touched Us
by Jennifer Aldrich

My mother passed away about three years ago. She was a huge believer in angels. I did not start to believe in them until she got cancer and was dying. A few months after she passed on, I started having dreams with her in them, and my sister would have a similar dream within a couple of days, before or after me.

One dream, in particular, touched both my husband and me. I had this dream right after we bought our first house and moved in. In the dream, we were settling into bed, and across from our bed was a piano. I had just fallen asleep and was awakened by the piano playing music and a white foggy light.

The light "stood up" and came over the bed. I saw my mom's face, and she just smiled very big at me. Then she reached out and touched my hand and my husband's hand. I woke up right after that. I had really felt her touch, and I was crying. When I told my husband about the dream, he said that he, too, had felt my mother touch his hand.

She has not been back since. I do miss her greatly, but I know she is home in heaven where she wanted to be.

※※※

It's Not Good-bye
by Jamee Harrison

My husband died on June 30, 1999. The very next evening, I had a very real dream about my husband, unlike any other dream I've ever had. The dream was very detailed, giving me every description of my husband as he was in this life with me.

In the dream, he was dressed like normal and was on a gurney at the morgue. I approached him and was talking to him, hoping he could hear every word I said. I told him how much I loved him and how much our two young daughters and I were going to miss him. As I lay down across his chest, I rubbed his face, bent down, gave him a kiss, and told him good-bye. At that point, his eyes opened and he sat up on the gurney.

I panicked and began walking backwards, away from him. I looked at the mortician and my sister-in-law, and asked, "What's happening?" The mortician told me that it was okay, because he was dead. I said, "How can he be dead? He opened his eyes and sat up on the table!"

My husband, Patrick, got up and started walking toward me with open arms, telling me to come here. I was so afraid that I continued to walk backwards until I ran into the wall. Patrick walked up to me and put his arms around me and held me and then said, "What do you

mean good-bye? It will never be good-bye. I will always be with you in your heart, spirit, and mind." At that point, I woke up in tears and could not go back to sleep.

A couple days later, on the day of my husband's memorial service, I was lying in bed with my eyes closed, but I was awake. I heard some light footsteps on the floor heading toward my bed. I then felt my bedcovers rustle as if someone had sat down on the edge. Thinking it was my grandmother waking me up, I opened my eyes, but there was no one there. I felt that Patrick was very close, and I have longed to have that feeling ever since.

Two months later, I had another very real dream about my husband, with the exact same message as the first dream, but this time I was at the airport in the bathroom washing my hands. I felt that someone was watching me, and when I turned to look, there stood my husband. I rubbed my eyes to make sure I wasn't seeing things. He said, "I'm here, and you aren't imagining me. I am as clear to you now as I was when I was in my physical body. I will always be with you." Since then, I have not had any more dreams about him, and I'm hoping I do very soon so that I'll know that he is still here with me.

❦❦❦

Everything Will Be Fine
by Kimberly Miller

After my grandmother's death, my father and I had the duty of cleaning out her apartment, which contained so many memories and brought back the immense feelings of loss. One evening, after having worked in her apartment sorting through things, I went home exhausted—not only from the cleaning, but from the emotions attached. My prayer before going to sleep was to have God help me accept that my grandmother was in a much better place. That night, I had the most realistic dream of my life.

In the dream, I was with my dad, cleaning and packing in my grandmother's apartment. All of a sudden, she walked out of her bedroom and sat at the kitchen table. I looked at her and said, "You're not supposed to be here. You're dead." Her reply was, "I know, but I just had to tell you that everything will be just fine, and I'll always be around." After saying this, she walked back to her bedroom. I woke up feeling a great deal of frustration over the dream, but realized that my grandmother came back to tell me she was all right so that I could move on.

He Held on to My Sister
by Teresa

My sister was struck by a car on December 1, 1999. She had been hit from behind and flew up on the driver's car before landing on the ground. After extensive testing, the doctor advised us that she was physically okay, but had sustained a traumatic brain injury. She was thought to be in danger of losing her life, and he was unable to provide us with any answers regarding her outcome or the effects of the injury. He said that this type of injury is usually "lethal" at the time. Everyone we knew began praying for her recovery, which I know helped her get through the ordeal. She was taken off the ventilator the next day and was able to speak to and recognize everyone. She remained in the hospital for one week and was sent to a rehab hospital to work on the few deficits (left-sided weakness and difficulty concentrating) she had remaining. She was released from the rehab hospital on December 30, 1999, three weeks earlier than originally planned.

One other miracle occurred, besides the fact that everyone's prayers assisted her in healing. The weekend before the accident, my sister told me about a dream she'd had about our brother who'd passed away in December of 1998. She said that the dream upset her to the point that she woke up crying. In the dream, my brother was in an airplane, which was odd because he never flew. He was also holding an infant.

Suddenly, the airplane started to crash. Throughout the crash, my brother continued to hold the infant tight to him. In the end, everyone in the airplane died, except for my brother and the infant. At the time, we did not understand what this meant, but I believe we do now. My sister is 12 years younger than my brother (he was 40 when he passed away). She is the baby of the family, and to him, she was still his baby sister. I truly do believe that my brother was my sister's guardian angel the day she was hit by the car, and he was protecting her from as much bodily injury as possible by holding her in his arms. I have always believed that we all have guardian angels who help protect us, but I feel that my sister is a testimonial to the fact that they do exist.

A Message from the Other Side
by Christine Lamberth

My husband and I were going through a very trying time in our relationship, so on this one particular night, I prayed like never before for help. When I fell asleep, I dreamed that I was on a beach with a man in a wetsuit. I wanted to talk with him, but there was a fence separating us. I informed him that I wanted to cross over and did not know how. He told me that all I had to do was put out the thought and trust, so I did, and I was lifted to the other side. Once I was standing before him, I proceeded to tell him who I was. He patiently listened to me, before telling me he knew who I was and that I was pregnant with a child.

While on the other side of the fence, I requested his help for my husband; however, he told me he could not interfere. He said that my husband was learning lessons and was on his own path. With that final message, I woke up and shared this dream with my husband, who informed me that his father had died 15 years ago while diving with him in the ocean.

It turned out just like my husband's father had told me in the dream—I really was pregnant at the time. I had a little boy, and we named him Christopher. This dream has given me faith in angels as our guardians.

I'm So Much Better Now
by Elizabeth Morton

About three years ago, Marcia, a friend with whom I played in the church handbell choir, was diagnosed with a terminal illness. She was given only a few months to live. I was very upset because Marcia was such a wonderful person—just a delight to be around. As she became sicker, I didn't go to visit her with the rest of the people from church. I guess I was scared of seeing her that way.

When I got the news that Marcia had passed away, I was extremely upset, mainly because I hadn't gone to visit her. I also missed her funeral because I was away at college in another state at the time. A few days after the funeral, I had the most beautiful dream. I was at church playing handbells. Marcia came up to me and gave me a hug and said, "Please don't worry about me. I'm fine. I'm so much better now." And then I woke up.

I really believe that she came to me to tell me not to worry about her anymore, and not to feel guilty about not visiting her. The dream was so real and so beautiful that I can't believe that it wasn't really her.

Making the World a Brighter Place
by Lee Lahoud

It was November of 1987, and it had been a really awful year for me. I was going through a really ugly divorce, my mother was dying of brain cancer, and I was having some very real and serious problems with her husband. I was on my way to see Mama, for what I knew would be one of the last times. Sometimes she knew me; sometimes she didn't.

My friend was driving me because I couldn't bear the thought of going there alone. It was a cold, gray, rainy day, and I was just miserable. Suddenly, all of the colors seemed to get brighter, and a very happy man just popped into my head. There is no other way to explain it. He was just there in my head, and the whole world seemed happy and much brighter.

He told me his name was Daniel, and he just wanted to say, "Hi," that better days were coming, and that I would be fine. Then he was gone. It was all very sudden and quick. I didn't have a clue who he was or what had just happened, but it seemed that the colors were still brighter, like someone had cleaned everything with window cleaner. I felt so much better. Whoever Daniel was, he had given me hope when I desperately needed it and couldn't find it within myself.

Two years later, I met a man named Russ at a Halloween party. In our very first conversation, not ten minutes after we met, he told me about his best friend, a spiritual man who had tried to live a totally intuitive life, and who had died in May of 1987. His name was Daniel. When I saw his photograph, I knew without a doubt that this was the Daniel who had given me hope that cold, rainy November day in 1987. Russ is now my husband.

❃ ❃ ❃

CHAPTER NINE

Angels Entering Dreams and Meditations

The Big Blue Angel of Peace and Healing
by H. Titus

It has been almost seven years since the passing of my beloved grandmother. I grew up with her; she was my other mother. So many days, I remember running across the field to her house just to watch her make cookies or to watch the TV game show *Classic Concentration* with her on the little black-and-white countertop TV set.

I would always go to Grandma's house with the excuse of wanting to dust for the quarter she gave me. We both knew that the real excuse was that we loved each other's company.

I remember the day of her funeral, and like a movie in my mind, I still see myself as the last one standing there at her grave as everyone left. Numb with grief, I had no tears to cry, no feeling anywhere. That day, and the feeling of being alone, has always haunted me.

Sometime later, I had a day where I felt especially alone and desolate. I took the day off of work and drove to the small graveyard in the small town in the countryside where my grandmother was buried. When I got there, I sat next to the headstone and cried for the first time since her death. I admitted that I was angry with God. Why did someone I loved have to die of such awful cancer? Why were children hurt? What did she do to deserve this? What did *I* do to deserve this? But no answers came, and I left the cemetery feeling just as alone as I'd felt days before.

That night, I had a very powerful dream: With my back to the headstone, and my head bent crying to God, I could see a big blue, beautiful angel over my left shoulder, watching me from over the headstone. I knew upon waking up that my grandma was in a better place, and that all was as it should be, even if I did not understand why. That dream, although simple, left me with a great feeling of peace and love.

❦❦❦

Dreams of Divine Guidance
by Sandara Smith

I was in Santa Fe, attending a class about massage therapy and spirituality. That night, I got a strong urge to call my mother and check on my father. When Mom got on the phone, she told me that Dad was ill, and that she was taking him to a cancer clinic in Temple, Texas, within the next few days. I am still amazed that I called home at that time, but I feel that the spiritual work I had been doing in my class opened me up to my angels' guidance.

The next evening, I returned home to Arizona, and I had my first dream encounter with angels. The two angels in my dream were very tall, with wings. They were white, with gold light emanating from their wings and bodies. I got the impression that they were very strong male angels. I only recall the face of one of them, and it was dimmed by the shine of the gold light coming off him.

Many weeks later in another dream, the same two angels told me I needed to fly to Dad's hospital in Temple in the morning. The words I heard didn't actually come from their lips, as much as a knowing what they were communicating. Nothing like this had ever happened to me before. I wasn't even sure why I was leaving in the morning, and neither was my husband. I contacted someone to watch my children, and then I was off. When I arrived at the hospital, I found my mother on a pay phone making a call to tell me that my father had brain cancer and they were to operate in the next few days. She would have been all alone if I hadn't flown in.

My father had the surgery, and it was worse than we had anticipated. The doctors said he wouldn't survive much more that two to four months. That night, the angels came again. This time, they asked me to get my children and move from Arizona to Dad's home in Oklahoma for the summer. The doctors hadn't even mentioned the next moves they would like to take, and the thought of a long hot summer in Oklahoma was anything but pleasant. Plus, I had been abused by this man as a child, and I wasn't really sure that I wanted to give to him what I felt I had missed out on.

The next morning, the doctors informed us that Dad had two options. Take him home and let him die within two months, or put him in a nursing home and do chemo and hope for four months. I knew what my answer was, so I told my mom, "See you in Oklahoma. I'll get my children and fly there and set the house up." The next few months were like spending time in a personal group therapy program. I spent hours releasing past ills by asking Dad questions about his earlier behavior. I would never have gotten the answers and the healing that accompanied them had I not followed the angels' guidance.

Toward the end of the two months, I decided to go on a vacation with my husband and children. We headed to the beach for a wonderful and much-needed rest. However, one night during our vacation, the angels came to me in my dreams again. They told me I needed to go to Oklahoma in the morning. When I called my mom the next morning to tell her I would be coming, she told me that Dad had gone into a coma that night.

I arrived in Oklahoma the next day. That night, for the first time in the entire two months I had been in Oklahoma, my sister, mother, and I were all together. All at once, the room seemed to change. A feeling of great energy filled the area around us, and Dad passed on.

I can't tell you why I followed the angels. Until that time, I never remember hearing from them. The gift I received because I did follow them was priceless, though. I picked up pieces of a soul that I desperately needed. I reconnected with a man whom I had been very angry with for a long time. Now I think of him with great love and affection and find that I even thank him for the childhood I had. I was helped by God and the angels' loving guidance to learn what an important person I was, and that my challenging beginnings made me the loving individual I am today.

❦❦❦❦

The Golden Cord
by Gerborg Frick

Three years ago, I participated in a workshop and was eventually initiated as a Reiki Master. During the final ceremony, we were encouraged to meditate and contemplate on our individual Reiki guardian. An angel appeared to me with shoulder-length blond hair, wearing a flowing garment with a golden cord around the waist. I could not distinguish the face or gender. The angel was very tall, at least seven feet.

Ending the meditation hour, everyone was asked to share their experience. Heather from Pennsylvania spoke first, and she described "my" angel in detail, saying, "The angel had a golden sash around the middle." I'm thinking, *No, it's not a sash; it's a cord,* and Heather instantly corrected herself and said, "Actually, it was a golden cord."

The group asked about the wings. We both gave our impression of the angels' wings, with the conclusion that they had nothing to do with feathers or flying, but were emanations of arched energy flowing in pastel rainbow colors. The astounding thing was that we both seemed to have encountered the same type of angel.

❦❦❦

The Pink Sponge Roller
by Cheryl Cash

We were reared to be strict Catholics. We went to church every Sunday and to confession every Saturday. Saturday evenings at sunset, we would recite the rosary.

We were raised at that time in military housing. We were bussed to Catechism by the military with other children of military parents. The Catechism was just like regular school; the nuns were strict, and they seemingly disliked children. School was difficult, and having to report to strict nuns at Catechism on Saturday mornings added to my despair in life. However, I did pay very close attention to their stories on how to be a good and helpful child.

I learned from one of my nuns that we could pray *anywhere*— not just at home or in church. We could pray simply for the sake of praying, and not just because we were asking for something. I rather liked the idea that I could pray wherever I was. I was quite fond of riding my bike and roller skating. I would think about what that nun said about praying, and I would stop my bike and begin reciting the Hail Mary and the Our Father in earnest, not caring if anyone saw.

Within this same time period, I began having dreams of angels hovering over me in my bed. They would talk with me and pick me up out of bed and fly me to all parts of the house. Sometimes I would wake up on the floor instead of in my bed. I wanted so much to believe that this was actually happening, because when I would wake up, it felt so real.

During one dream where the angels were carrying me, I dropped one of my pink sponge rollers while in flight on the third step at the bottom of our staircase. The following morning, there on the third step lay one of my pink sponge rollers. I was so excited, but I told no one because I knew that nobody would believe me.

(w)(w)(w)

An Empowering Dream
by Anonymous

I had a very powerful and memorable dream. In it, I saw a beautiful pink lily flower, a stargazer. Suddenly, out of the middle of the flower, a gorgeous fairy appeared. She shimmered and sparkled, and looked at me and said, "You can have anything you want. You just have to ask for it and then believe that you can have it." I woke up feeling very peaceful and empowered, and the feeling returns whenever I recall the dream.

)€)€)€

CHAPTER TEN

Seeing Angel Lights

The Choice
by Christine Sinon

When I was pregnant with my first child, I lived on a small island in Micronesia, Ponape. I got up to use the outhouse in the middle of the night. Nobody else in the house was awake. I left the door ajar because it always got stuck, and I didn't want to wake everybody up when I came back. As I returned to the house, I felt a silence around me, as if I were separated from the house. The door was closed and locked—at least *I* couldn't open it—but nobody was awake inside. I tapped lightly, thinking that whoever closed the door would still be awake and let me in, but nobody stirred and nobody heard me. It was as if we were separated by some invisible barrier. I walked around to the back door. I looked in our bedroom window and tried to wake my husband.

Once in the backyard, I felt a multitude of spiritual presences around and above me, not threatening in any way, but perhaps curious. I saw many points of light that looked like stars, but they were very close to me in the night sky, probably about six feet off the ground (I am 5'3" tall), and I felt as if the spirits were just slightly above my head. Although I didn't see anything concrete, I somehow knew that they were spirits of dead relatives of my husband.

I felt that they were asking if I wanted one of them to be reincarnated as the soul for the baby I was carrying. At the time, I did not believe in reincarnation. I tried to shrug these feelings off and attempted to get back in the house. I knocked louder and even called out, but the people in the house didn't hear me. I felt that if I didn't make some kind of choice, I would be stuck outside all night. I was starting to feel scared.

Finally, I said aloud, "I don't want any of you. I don't even know any of you. You're being too pushy. I'll take someone who's sitting up there in a corner somewhere who gave up ever having another chance at life on Earth a long time ago!" And in that instant, the night sounds returned. I walked to the front door, and it was ajar, just as I had left it. And the next morning, nobody admitted to having gotten up, closed, locked, and then opened the door.

Healing Lights
by Birgitte Suhr

Our five-year-old daughter was not well—her ear was hurting her. We were in my bed, and she was crying. I held my hand on her ear and asked for help from the light. At that instant, the bed was encircled by a lot of silent white shadows. I felt a warmth in my hand, and I noticed a pink shine radiating from some shadows. My daughter stopped crying, and the room became very peaceful. I don't know how long it lasted, but the shadows disappeared as peacefully as they had come.

The next morning, our daughter was well again. Her ear did not hurt anymore. I think that the lights and shadows were angels, and I believe they came to tell me about healing.

Lights of Purity and Joy
by Jonathan Robinson

Several years ago, some friends and I went to the Anza Borrego desert, about 100 miles east of San Diego. Our plan was to spend several days hiking and meditating. After a day of hiking, we found a very remote spot and started to set up camp for the night.

My spiritual teacher had told me that angelic beings sometimes visited this area, and that they could sometimes be attracted by the playing of music. He had given me and my friend wooden flutes to play, even though neither of us knew how to play them. He told us to find a place that felt comfortable and learn how to play a simple song together. We became very engrossed in trying to play our flutes. After about an hour, the air seemed to start vibrating around us. My friend and I looked up and saw five balls of light surrounding us. The lights were different colors and sizes, ranging from a couple feet to perhaps seven feet in diameter. At first I thought I was hallucinating, but then I saw my friend pointing to the same balls of light I was seeing. We were in awe.

The balls of light started to make childlike noises, as if they were playing with us by bouncing around our heads. They seemed to emanate a vibration of purity, innocence, and just plain fun.

❦❦❦

White Lights and the Miraculous Recovery
by Donna DeRuvo

My seven-year-old son, Joseph, was very ill. I was naturally very concerned about his recovery, and worried that he would have long-term permanent damage from his illness if his medication did not work. I prayed every day, asking God to send as many angels as possible to heal and protect him. I prayed that the

Archangel Raphael would send his green light of healing to surround Joseph. I prayed morning, noon, and night, always trying not to doubt, especially when I looked at Joseph's limp body sleeping in my bed.

One afternoon, Joey asked me to lie down with him, complaining of feeling worse than ever. He cried in pain, and I cried in fear. Again, I began to pray, stronger than ever before. As I closed my eyes, I began to see little white lights in the darkness. I assumed that there was something in my eyes, or that I was seeing things. I opened my eyes to focus and kept seeing these lights. I can't really describe it, but it was beautiful all around the room. I kept looking, not understanding what I saw. But as suddenly as they appeared, they disappeared.

The next day, Joey woke up feeling much better. He had a quick recovery, never having any lasting symptoms. I thank the angels and God.

❦❦❦

Illumination
by Lisa Crofts

On December 8, 1994, at 7:50 P.M., I was on my way to see a friend whom I had not seen in years. I was 23 years old. Just a week before, I had bought a beautiful bumper sticker that I had not yet put on my car, which read: "CAUTION: Never drive faster than your angels can fly!" Those words stood out in my mind so much that I was only going 5 miles over the 50 mile-per-hour speed limit.

Just as I approached the crest of a hill, a dark vehicle passed me going the opposite way. When I looked back in front of me, I saw a huge cloud of dirt. I then saw what I will never forget in my entire life! A car was coming at me broadside. I thought, *Oh my God, I'm going to die!*

At the moment just before impact, the other car became illuminated in a glorious white light, and I had a moment of clarity. I knew I would not die, but that the person in the other car *would*, and that I was going to be in a great deal of pain. The other car exploded on impact. My impact was hard, and fortunately I was wearing my seatbelt and had an airbag.

With flaming debris flying everywhere, I crawled out of my car's passenger side. I saw people burning in the other car. I had to help them! I took only a few steps when my legs gave out. I learned later that I had a broken ankle.

I watched helplessly as other passersby tried in vain to save the young man's life, but he burned to death there on the side of the road. He was only 24. It was later learned that he had been passing many cars, and when he tried to pass the last one, a race started because the dark vehicle got that "you can't pass me" attitude. That's where I came in, and my life changed forever.

It took me a while to understand the vision of the white light until I talked with the woman who had sold me the bumper sticker. She said that the white light was my angel helping me get through the trauma. What an amazing thought for me to comprehend. Not that I don't believe in angels, but nothing like that had ever happened to me! I know now that my vision helped me more than I can ever understand, and I will be forever grateful for my angels' help.

Escorted by Angels
by Elaine M. Elkins

My husband and I were flying to Reno, Nevada, for some fun. I am so terrified to fly that I always take a pill to calm me during a flight. On the Reno flight, though, I had forgotten to bring a pill with me. The flight was becoming progressively bumpier. I could feel the plane dropping altitude and then climbing. The pilot apologized for the turbulence and said he tried different altitudes, yet nothing was working. The flight crew was ordered to sit down and buckle up.

I told my husband that I was terrified, and I didn't think we were going to make it. He was the pillar of calm. I thought for sure that the plane was going to go down. I had never experienced anything like it, and I was so mad for forgetting to take my pill. He gave me a book to read to take my mind off the flight, but I wondered how anyone could read at such as time. He said, "You really need to read this book; it will help," and he handed me a copy of *Angel Therapy*.

I read that Raphael will come with you when you travel and help you arrive at your destination safely. So I silently told Raphael, "I am terrified, scared silly. Please be here to help this plane land safely." Still, I didn't feel anything but fear. Then I read that you can call a thousand angels, and they will be there. So I silently prayed, "I am really scared, I want to return home to my children. My daughter needs me. I need a thousand angels here. I need to know you are here."

I was staring out the window, and all of a sudden, I saw little bright dots on the window. At first, I thought it was that light you see out the side of your peripheral vision. So I stared. As I continued to look, I could see definite patterns of light coming up into a starburst and falling like fireworks, only to fall to the bottom of the window and then form another starburst.

I also saw the little dancing lights form a circle and spin. For the longest time, I watched these patterns on the windows. My husband asked what I was doing. I smiled and replied, "I'm watching the angels." I then felt that we were going to be okay. I watched the angels play for the rest of the flight and realized that the plane was going to make it. It did, thanks to Raphael and his band of angels.

We had a wonderful time in Reno with our friends. On the flight home, I kept staring at the window. It was a wonderful flight—no bumps, and people were talking. I realized that the reason I didn't see the lights was because I felt safe and knew we would be home soon. The angels were there, and they were wonderful.

❦❦❦

Steam Room Angels
by Stephanie Gunning

Last year, I learned a new way to pray, and because I am an endless experimenter, I wanted to test how effective it was. It's not that I am a spiritual skeptic, it's just that I got excited. I had been told there are four important steps to prayer. First, find a sanctuary. Second, breathe into the prayer. Third, admit your vulnerability; and fourth, ask for what you want or need as if your prayer has already been answered.

The next afternoon, I worked out at the gym and decided to take a steam bath. Lying on my back on a towel, alone and naked in the steam room, I remembered the list of prayer steps I'd just been taught. *Well, I couldn't find more of a sanctuary,* I thought. And for sure, I was in a vulnerable position. Plus, if I prayed in the dark, no one who entered the steam room would realize what I was doing; and while I was alone, I could talk out loud to make extra sure I was "doing it right."

I decided to pray for my soulmate to find me. I had indulged in the fantasy of finding a partnership similar to the one some friends of mine had, but my idealism was shattered when my friends divorced and the husband committed suicide. Since then, it seemed as if soulmates weren't real.

First, I breathed deeply into my body and admitted my vulnerability. "Dear God and Divine Mother," I prayed, "here I am. I am a woman alone in the world. There are so many reasons why." Then I listed my reasons. I added, "I am so very lonely sometimes."

I explained that I had lost my ideal of marriage, and I prayed for peace over the loss of my friend's life. I continued praying in minute detail, leaving nothing out.

All at once in the darkness, I almost felt a change of atmosphere. I was so intent on prayer and breath and being open-hearted that I had entered into an intense, highly focused state of being. Through the clouds of steam, with my eyes closed, I saw a pulsing, dark red spiral of energy envelop me. It was not frightening, but comforting. I burst into tears. Then there were shoots of bright green piercing the field of energy throbbing around me, and swirling mists of rich purple.

I intuitively knew that each light was a separate being, and it was so humbling that they had come to be with me in my time of need and vulnerability. I felt tremendously connected to the Divine, and I knew without a doubt that the light was a friend who had come to reassure me. I felt entirely loved by heaven's angels.

Once connected, I continued my prayer, which became a statement of gratitude for my soulmate, who I know will find me. I believe it. Since that day, I haven't felt lonely or anxious about the future and love. I look everyone in the eyes to see their soul and establish a clear connection. When my soulmate arrives, on or behind schedule, or even if I miss him here on Earth this time around, that's okay. As my steam-room angels helped me understand, love is everywhere.

Saved by the Light
by Mili Ponesse

I was driving home from work one day. I was 16 years old and had just received my driver's license. I stopped at a red light and was in a hurry. I impatiently waited for the light to turn green so that I could take off quickly.

All of a sudden, though, I lost focus of that traffic light. From out of nowhere, a bright light similar to sun glare brought my attention to the side of the road. I just sat there, transfixed by the light, almost daydreaming, but not thinking of anything. I was startled when the driver behind me honked his horn. The traffic light had turned green, and I hadn't noticed.

However, before I could collect myself, a truck flew through the red light, crossing my path at about 70 miles an hour. If I'd gone through that light as soon as it turned green, I would have been hit by that speeding truck and been in an extremely bad accident.

I know that an angel saw the danger coming my way and distracted me with the bright light to keep me from driving through the intersection. I know it was an angel because of the comfort and warmth I felt for the rest of my "slow" ride home.

A Comforting Sight
by Branka M.

I believe that my angel or angels are around me, because whenever I am really upset about something, I see what appears to be sparkling bubbles. They are just above floor level, going up about three feet. The bubbles don't really float up or down; they're just there, and then they're gone. It's like sparkles appearing from nowhere. They're not there for any length of time.

The first time this happened to me, I intuitively knew not to be afraid, and actually felt comforted by them. My sister recently told me that she has had this exact vision from time to time.

A Stream of Shimmering Sparkles
by Cheri Bunker

One night right after I'd gone to bed, I opened my eyes and saw many small flashes of light streaking by. I closed my eyes and then opened them again, and I still saw the flashes. I told myself that this must be something of a Divine nature. All of a sudden, next to my bed I saw the most beautiful silver and gold shimmering sparkles coming down in a stream.

I told myself to be calm, because I know that if you are afraid of angels, they will not appear to you. I kept staring at this steady stream of light, and then I saw the outline of a very tall person. This lasted a few more minutes, and then it was gone. I felt very peaceful and unafraid.

Guardian on the Road
by Douglas Lockhart

My wife and I were truck drivers. One night, we were crossing the border between Arizona and New Mexico. My wife was lying down in the sleeper, and I was driving. It was about 3:00 A.M., and I was very tired, but there was no time to stop and sleep because our job required us to get the freight from point A to point B.

I continued to drive, and I don't know if I fell asleep at the wheel, but the next thing I knew, a great white ball of light came from the blackened night sky and passed through me. It blew my hair back, and I immediately felt as refreshed as if I had slept for ten hours. It was the most amazing thing that has ever happened to me.

A Validation of Faith
by Donald L. Murphy

One evening after reading Doreen's book *Angel Therapy*, I said the prayer that asked the angels to come into my life to remove all obstacles that were preventing me from enjoying myself. Being somewhat doubtful, I added, "Guardian angel, if you are real, please manifest yourself to me in the morning."

When I awoke the next morning, I saw beautiful gold shimmering light in my bedroom for a couple of seconds. The light then disappeared. This proved to me that angels are real and that I *do* have a guardian angel.

♥♥♥

The Light of My Mother's Love and Wisdom
by Judith Mitchell

I was 41 when my mother unexpectedly passed away. I was overwhelmed with grief and loss. Her passing made me realize that I was unsure of my own spiritual beliefs and that I did not like my feeling of aloneness. One night while I was trying to sleep, my mother came to me as a spinning ball of red light. I knew that it was her!

I could actually put my hand into this light. I was filled with such a sense of love. She let me know that I was never alone, and that she loved me and was always with me. Mom also let me know that the circle of life and love were very important, that there are many spirits around me all the time, and that life goes on. Mostly, she helped me understand that she was fine and happy.

My mother was raised a Catholic, and so many people had asked, "Was she saved?" Well, Mom let me know that we are *all* saved. That was not an issue. She helped me see that there are so many paths that lead to the same place. I had always fought my gift of seeing and knowing, and now I am so thankful to know that I am not alone, that life goes on, and that change is good. My mother's visit changed my life for the better and put me on a greater spiritual path. I know I may call on her any time.

I no longer feel the pain of missing her, for I know she is with me always. My whole outlook on life has improved now, and I am open to receiving the help that is there for me if I need it. The love is always there. I am so grateful for this wonderful glimpse of the afterlife that I've been given. I thank God for it.

A Reassuring Mist
by Violet Burns

It happened about 28 years ago when I came home from the midnight shift at the post office. My family members were standing in the yard when I pulled up to my waterfront home. They said, "Don't get excited, Mother, but Billy and his friend didn't come home from the bay, and we have the Coast Guard out looking for them."

I started to scream, but I saw a heavy mist fall on me, and its presence calmed me down. I then heard these words that were spoken to me: "Billy will be home in 20 minutes."

I saw a boat coming after 15 minutes, and he was home in another 5 minutes. That was the greatest miracle I've ever experienced.

Inseparable
by Eileen Straley

My mother, Jayne Warren, had been a smoker all of her adult life. In August 1998, she was diagnosed with lung cancer. Six weeks later, she passed on. My father, Floyd Warren, and my sister went to the funeral home to make arrangements for her, since I lived in a different state. As my father left the funeral home, he fell off the cement steps and landed on his head. He went to the hospital and had brain surgery. Afterward, Dad required 'round-the-clock care in his home. He responded very well to his physical therapy, and we talked every day.

While the care giver was with him on the morning of February 9, 1999, there was a flash of light in the darkened room. My father looked over the shoulder of the care giver and said, "Hello, Jayne, I've missed you so," and then he fell over dead. My mother, I believe, had come back to get Daddy. They had been married for more than 42 years.

❀❀❀

An Urgent Message from the Mist
by Gerborg Frick

My angel story has to do with my something that happened to my son when he was 4 years old (he's now 31). It was early April, and we lived by a lagoon of one of Michigan's 10,000 lakes. It had been so cold the previous night that a thin sheet of ice covered the lagoon.

My youngster, always active, was anxious to go outside. I bundled up and firmly told him, "Martin, do not go near the ice on the lagoon, do you hear?" His beautiful light blue eyes shone at me in trust, and without a reply, out he went.

I sat down at the table near the picture window overlooking the lake and got busy with my knitting machine, which soon had my mind focused on it. All of a sudden, I looked up into a white mist that hovered above my table. I looked into the kitchen to see if something was boiling and creating steam. But nothing was on. I smelled the air for smoke to see if something was burning and creating the white cloud hovering above my table, but no smoke was in the air.

Baffled, I looked at the white mist again, and it was now stretching and stretching toward the window. I looked out and saw Martin in the middle of the lagoon on that thin sheet of ice.

Horrified, I jumped up and ran outside on the balcony, hollering, "Martin, get in at once!" The child obeyed, and he was saved. That ice would not have carried me. Later, I had time to ponder the mist. I am convinced it was a guardian angel or spirit that sought my attention.

Thank You, God
by Anita Pyle

On April 19, 1999, I was driving through a long area of road construction. Traffic was snarled by the bottleneck created by the construction. I was stopped behind an 18-wheeler truck, and the next thing I knew, I was waking up and could see the sky. I didn't know where I was or what had happened, but I saw shattered glass everywhere around me. To my right was the bed of the 18-wheeler, no more than a foot from my head. Before I completely regained consciousness, though, I saw this beautiful white light.

I realized I'd been in an accident and that my neck was broken. I smelled the stench of gasoline; and my head, neck, back, and legs really hurt. I knew my life had been changed forever. Then I started smelling chemicals. The car that had hit me had a flatbed trailer that carried three 50-gallon barrels of chemicals. One barrel had fallen off, and its contents were now spilling out, mixing with the gas. The smell was overwhelming.

Someone put a cloth over my nose and mouth and told me not to take it off. Everyone around me said they had to get me out, since they were afraid that the car would explode. But they couldn't get me out—I was trapped. The ambulance and fire trucks had to use the "Jaws of Life" to rescue me. I was then airlifted to the hospital.

I later found out that the car that rear-ended me pushed the back end of my car into the back seat. My car was pushed into the 18-wheeler, which tore the roof off of my car. The only place in my car that wasn't damaged was right where I was sitting. If anyone else had been with me that day, they would have been killed. Everyone that saw my car said that my guardian angel must have saved me, as I should have been killed.

I had a fish symbol on the trunk lid of my car. All around the fish symbol, my car was completely crushed and dented, but the little symbol was not scratched or broken. My brother removed the fish symbol from my car, and I now carry it in my wallet. I am still in a lot of pain, but I thank God daily for saving my life. I know He has a job for me to do here on this old earth. I praise Him every chance I get. I love to show the pictures of my car to people and tell them how God saved my life. Everyone agrees that my angel was there with me that day.

❍❍ ❍❍ ❍❍

CHAPTER ELEVEN

Seeing Signs from Above

The Purple-Haired Angel
by Leanne Hernandez

My grandmother died in 1998, shortly before my daughter's fifth birthday. In her younger days, my grandmother was known for being quite eccentric—she had even dyed her hair lavender for many years.

I was out of town on a business trip, so my mother helped me get ready for my daughter's birthday party by ordering a cake with a brunette angel on it. When she went to pick up the cake, she was amazed to find that the baker had used lavender icing for the angel's hair. My mother asked, "Who ever heard of an angel with purple hair?" I knew that this was my grandmother's way of telling us that she had made it to heaven and was with us in spirit to celebrate my daughter's special day.

Angel on My Shoulder
by Gerri Magee

I was at the Church of Today in Warren, Michigan, attending a workshop with Doreen Virtue on communicating with God and our guardian angels. Before the lunch break, Doreen told us that we all come into this life with at least two guardian angels, one on our left and one on our right side. Doreen had us close our eyes, be silent, and listen to the guardian angels tell us their names.

The room was quiet as we closed our eyes. We were instructed to listen to the voice of the angel on our left side. Surprisingly, I heard a voice gently whisper, "Gabriel," and felt a soft, light touch on that side. As we continued to sit in the silence, Doreen told us to trust the voice that we'd heard. Then we were to tune in to the voice of the angel on our right side. The voice that I heard this time was a bit stronger, and I felt a little pressure on my right shoulder as I heard the name "Michael" called out.

We all continued sitting in silence for several minutes, then Doreen had us all come back to the present moment. She then asked if everyone got a name from their angels. As we were leaving for lunch, Doreen asked us to look for a sign that would confirm the names that we had received.

So we all left the room and went out to lunch. At the restaurant, I was seated across from a friend, talking with her about the workshop we were attending, when out of the corner of my eye, I noticed something on my right shoulder. "What's this?" I asked as I reached around with my left hand and literally had to dislodge it from the material of my dress. I couldn't believe my eyes. What I saw was a small fluffy-white feather. It was embedded in the shoulder area of my dress. My friend and I both gasped as we realized that that was the shoulder where I heard the name "Michael" called out. Here was the sign I'd asked for—a white feather as proof of my angel.

I was so excited that I ran over to two other tables in the restaurant where other people from the workshop were sitting. I just had to show them this special sign. They were all wowed by it. Imagine the joy of finding a feather stuck on your shoulder as a sign from the Divine world of angels! Now that's got to be proof enough for almost anyone that angels really do exist, and they do answer our requests. After all, everyone in the room had heard their angels' names called out to them as well, and had received signs. Even though we can't see them, they *are* there.

Then at the end of the day, Doreen told us to again sit quietly and our angels would give us a message. The room became silent, and as I closed my eyes, the angel on my right side (Michael) did give me a message. He whispered, "You are loved." He repeated it again, and I felt enveloped in what felt like wings surrounding me and enfolding me inside. "You are loved."

I will always feel the presence of my angels and remember hearing them, too. I believe that I now have a strong personal connection with my angels. The reason I'm sharing this with you is to let you know that your angels are always here with you, waiting for you to ask for their assistance in any given situation. Never doubt that you have guardian angels; you are never alone.

The Comforting Angel Cloud
by Rebecca Powers

My father was dying of cancer. It was near the end, and we had him at home, comfortable and in no pain. He was comatose, but I knew that he was aware we were with him. I was having a hard time dealing with the whole "death" thing, and I was afraid for him—afraid of what he was feeling, and afraid of what he was about to go through. I wanted to make sure he would be okay and not alone, but I needed some sort of answer, some sort of sign. I had none, and I was afraid.

It was a typical October night, and my family and I were waiting for the end, *praying* for the end. I went out on the front step to get some fresh air with a friend who was comforting me. I sat down and said a little prayer. I pleaded, "Please, please, give me some sort of sign, any sign, just so I'll know he'll be okay."

At that very moment, I looked into the sky at the beautiful sunset, and I saw an angel—plain as day, clear to my human eyes. It was a beautiful cloud—a beautiful angel. There was my answer.

I ran inside, got my mother, and grabbed a camera. We both sat there and wept. I took a picture of the angel, then she disappeared. My father passed away ten minutes later. The angel had come to take him home. At that point I knew, I really *knew* . . . that he was okay. My father was not alone, and he was with that beautiful angel going home. I have the picture of the angel and will send it to anyone who doesn't believe. I believe. I will *always* believe.

Instant Validation
by Marie Nelson

I heard about an angel store called "Tara's Angel" in San Juan Capistrano, California. I went to the store and wandered around for about an hour. I really didn't believe in angels, but I was willing to see what this was all about. The store did have a wonderful feeling, and I heard lots of angel stories while in there. *Well,* I started thinking, *maybe there are angels with us.* As I walked to my car, I silently asked the Lord to send me a sign if there really were angels around us. I drove off, got on the freeway, and within three minutes, a car pulled in front of me with a license plate that read "RAPHAEL." Was this a message, or what?

Happy in Heaven
by Helen

My 24-year-old son died on August 14, 1999. His presence is sorely missed, as he had lived at home with us while attending college. Thoughts of my son consume my mind almost every moment of every given day, even though I am wholly functioning.

One evening shortly after Thanksgiving, I was having a very difficult moment while alone in my home. I was drawn to the window, since the container holding my son's ashes was sitting on the window seat. (We were going to be spreading his ashes on the ocean soon.) As I put my fingertips on the container, missing him and talking to him while softly crying, I noticed that the moon was very low in the sky and extremely bright.

For the short time I was standing by the window, I suddenly became aware that a cloud appeared as the outline of a complete angel with large rounded wings on each side of a delicate body wearing a flowing gown, as feetlike clouds formed that hung below the gown! It was a most comforting sight for me, and I felt momentarily at peace. I had a sense that my son, who probably feels for me, was trying to relay that he is with the angels and that they are taking good care of him in heaven.

♥♥♥

An Inner Certainty
by Lucie Grace Fuller-Kling

I am seven years old. I had a very unique experience of seeing my guardian angel. It happened this past Monday as our family drove back from our vacation in Canada. I was looking out the window at the clouds, and suddenly I saw an angel up in the sky. It looked like it was wearing a cloud silk dress fluttering in the wind. It had curly little ringlets in its hair, and its face looked like it was smiling at me. At that moment, something from deep down inside of me popped up into my head, and my body was telling me that it was a sign from my guardian angel.

❦❦❦

The Message from the Rose Petals
by Bonnie Suzanne Koester

I was having some difficulty at a small college where I worked. There was a lot of politics among the employees, including my boss, and things got so bad that I considered quitting my job. I prayed for guidance.

As was my routine, every morning I would go to the convenience store next to the college for breakfast. On this day, I found some red rose petals lying on the grass between the college and the store. I picked one up and smiled, inwardly asking, "Is this from my angels?" But then I concluded that someone must have thrown them there. I took one petal back to my office and placed it on the base of my lamp.

The next morning, I came in, and the petal had shriveled. I went to the store, and there on the grass in the same place were fresh pink rose petals. There was no sign of the red ones. I furrowed my brow and thought, *How could I have missed these yesterday, and who is doing this?* And why would someone be throwing rose petals on the ground? I was trying my best to think of a logical explanation.

I picked up one of the pink petals, and as I walked across the parking lot returning to my office, I smelled the scent of roses so strongly that it made my eyes widen. I thought, *A single petal would not give off this scent.* I raised my hand to my nose and smelled the petal. I smelled nothing but the scent of my hand. I took it away, and again there was that strong smell of roses!

Pasadena, Texas, where I live and work, has oil refineries. The air here never smells like roses. I knew beyond a shadow of a doubt that these were signs from my angels. Peace, calm, joy, love, and laughter that just makes you grin—that's the best way I can explain it.

I took this petal and placed it alongside the withered red one. The next day, the pink had withered as well. I returned once again to the spot, and there I found both red and pink petals, and they were fresh. With a smile, I said, "Okay, okay, I'll tough it out. I'll stay here a bit longer. Thank you. You guys are too much!"

They were right—I now have a new position at the college and have almost doubled my income. And I still have the petals.

❦❦❦

Sign of the Rainbow
by Danielle

I was returning from a family vacation, feeling very dejected and alone. It was such a low point in my life that I was on the verge of contemplating suicide,

I looked over and saw a double rainbow in the sky, which was strange because it hadn't rained that day. I asked my mother if she saw it, but she didn't. Neither had my brother. I knew that this was a sign just for me, because I heard a voice say, "Everything is going to work out fine. Everything will be okay. You are loved, Danielle. God loves you."

This voice and this vision changed my life from that point on. The depression lifted, and I began my search to help others who were in my situation heal and grow. I can honestly say that I am a new person now because I know that I am loved. The old ego-driven thoughts and fears are gone.

❦❦❦

A Sign of Protection
by Micci DeBonis

My mother, Katherine, had just purchased a new car, so for good luck, I had given her an angel clip that went on the visor in the car.

On this particular day, my mother was watching my six-month-old daughter for the day while I was at work. While on an outing in Mom's new car, they stopped for gasoline.

They were waiting in line at the gas pumps, and my daughter was making a fuss in the back seat. My mother turned to see what the problem was and noticed that my daughter needed her bottle, so she turned around to get it. Right then, she noticed a car coming straight toward her! The man hit the front of Mom's car, completely totaling it. The air bag deployed, and luckily she wasn't hurt and neither was my baby.

After the police reports were completed, Mom went back to the car and noticed that the angel clip was missing from the sun visor. Looking all over the car, she finally found the clip: It had landed in the back seat where my daughter was in her car seat. I truly believe that angels played a part in the safety of my mother and my daughter. The police officer said if my mother had been a couple of feet closer to the tanks, the outcome would not have been very good.

There were angels around my mother and daughter during that ordeal, and she and I thank them every day.

❦❦❦

A Sign from the Blessed Mother
by Antoinette Voll

My mom, age 66, was having a hard time breathing whenever she climbed stairs or walked up hills. It got to the point where it was getting more and more difficult. Since I had lost my dad just 18 months earlier, we were all walking on eggshells. She finally had medical tests conducted that showed that she had two coronary blockages. Our family doctor referred my mom to a hospital where they could perform an exploratory procedure to see the extent of her blockage.

One week before, I started praying earnestly to the Blessed Mother. I would talk to her picture and pray that she would either make the blockages disappear or please give me strength to handle this next crisis. So when my mother went to the hospital that morning, her sister stayed with me, and we prayed.

When the procedure was over, the doctor at the hospital asked why my mother was having this test. The exploratory procedure showed that her arteries were in perfect condition, with no blockage whatsoever. I told him to ask our family doctor. When our family doctor came down, they all had the strangest looks. There was no logical answer.

As the attendants were wheeling my mother down to the hospital ward, they found out that all the beds were taken and they had to put her at the nurse's station. As they parked her near the window of the station, right above her head was the same picture of the Blessed Mother that I had prayed to all week. Did my spirits ever soar! It was the most amazing feeling. We truly witnessed a miracle, and the Blessed Mother showed me her picture to reassure me that she had intervened!

Daniel
by Charmaine Jabr

My 44-year-old brother, Daniel, passed away from liver illness. He had abused drugs and alcohol all of his adult life, and as a result, made some terrible mistakes that affected many people.

I loved him just the same, and always wondered what happened to his soul when he died.

It was around the time of his birthday, and Elton John's song "Daniel" was on the car radio. Hearing my brother's name in the song's title and lyrics brought me to tears. I begged God to give me a sign to let me know what happened to Dan's soul. Well, just then, a pickup truck pulled up in front of me and had the most awesome mural painted on it. On the left side of the tailgate was a dark, stormy, dreary-looking scene, and on the right side was Jesus floating up in the clouds into heaven. Then I read the license plate frame, which said, "Jesus Won."

From that day on, the immense grief I felt over the loss of my brother was lifted. His childhood was filled with so much pain that the odds were against him from the start. He suffered terribly in this life, yet he had such spirit and charm that he could only be somewhere better. Now I know that for sure.

Bless You!
by Cammi Collier

My husband and I went to Sedona, Arizona, Christmas week. We were taking a walk one night, and the moon was brilliant and comforting. However, I was cold, and my nose was running! I said to my husband, "I know this angel stuff works when I'm alone. Let's see if it works with *you* here, too!"

I said a prayer for a tissue to blow my nose. I've learned that no request is too trivial for the angels. Right away, I heard the angels tell me to look toward the right side of the road. Sure enough, about three feet ahead of us on the right side of the road were two clean facial tissues. Although I believe in miracles, I am still thrilled when I witness them. The tissues were new, thick, and soft, with a lotion scent.

I thanked the angels for their love and generosity. It's comforting to know that they can even take care of runny noses!

An Abundant Sign
by Elles Taddeo

Several years ago, my husband had some frightening physical symptoms, and we were very concerned that his condition might be serious. He was scheduled to go to the doctor and have some medical tests performed. One afternoon when I was at the park with my son, I felt especially worried about my husband's health. I asked my guardian angel to let me know if everything would be okay.

I said to the angels, "Please let me find a four-leaf clover as a sign that things are fine with my husband." I sat down in the grass with my son, looked down, and there was my four-leaf clover! I picked it and happily showed it to my son. Then I looked down again at the same spot, and there was another four-leaf clover. Delighted, I picked it up and remarked how unusual this was. I pointed to the spot where it came from to show my son, and we saw another one! And another one and another! I picked a total of 27 four-leaf clovers from the same little patch of grass! The next day, I found five more in my own backyard! I dried them all and still have them.

The angels must have thought something like, *Okay, you want a four-leaf clover, you'll get four-leaf clovers!* Although I later tried to find my magic patch again, I never could. Needless to say, all my husband's tests went fine, and there was nothing wrong with him.

All You Have to Do Is Ask
by Reta

It had been a really busy day. I had an interview for a position that I truly felt was mine, but there were some obstacles that would have to be overcome along the way. I took a vacation day, had a mid-morning massage, came home, and prepared for the series of interviews to follow.

That evening, I had considerable trouble calming down. I knew that the next day would be truly grueling, complete with a nearly four-hour drive, two morning meetings, followed by another almost four hours on the road for a late-afternoon meeting, and another 90-minute drive back home. About the time I was giving up on falling asleep, I decided to visit Doreen Virtue's Website.

I'll never forget my visit to **www.angeltherapy.com.** I read an article Doreen wrote called "You Are Surrounded by Angels." I needed that reinforcement. I reread it and felt my composure return. As I walked away from my computer and went into my living room on my way to bed, I thought, *In some way, I have experienced every one of the angel manifestations about which Doreen spoke, but I don't remember finding any unexplained feathers. That would be a really awesome experience!*

The next morning came quickly. On my way out of town, I went to my office to write a thank-you note to the interviewers and pick up the files I would need that day. As I left my office, I was so confident that I locked the door without a second glance. A stop at the rest room was appropriate due to the length of the drive and the early hour. As I turned on the bathroom light, I noticed that there was something on my skirt. I was quite annoyed, because returning home and changing was going to cost about an hour's worth of time. I tried to brush off whatever it was . . . and stopped in my tracks—I realized that I was looking at feathers on my skirt!

Of course, this made me feel cared for and loved and supported. I had gotten my angel feathers, and all I had to do was ask.

CHAPTER TWELVE

Near-Death and Deathbed
Visions and Visitations

A Revealing Experience
by Chaya Kostelicki

My dad died on February, 24, 1991. Exactly four months later to the day, I suffered a cardiac arrest myself. I went through the light while being treated in the hospital. During this dream, hallucination, or whatever term you want to use for my experience, my dad and an old friend of mine came to talk to me. When I got out of the hospital, I called my dad's wife and asked her for this friend's phone number. She said that the friend had died, just prior to Christmas in 1990, unbeknownst to me.

❁❁❁

A Life-Changing Experience
by Tammy Zienka

In 1996, I was involved in a car accident with one other car that carried a family of four. I remember seeing the fear in their eyes immediately before their car crashed into the side of the automobile where I was seated. I was sure I was going to die, too.

The next thing I remember was being in a golden room with a long table with many golden light beings, one of whom was my dear grandfather. I was so happy! I was laughing—not because anything was funny, but because I was infinitely happy. At that moment, I remembered what my purpose on Earth was. I said to my Grandpa, who was there in the spirit world with me, "I can't believe I've allowed myself to worry so much about petty things!"

I don't remember anything else that was said to me in heaven. I mostly remember feelings and being with Grandpa Jim. Then, a being of light and I were suddenly back at the scene of the accident. Since it felt as though I'd been in the golden room for a long time, I didn't recognize the Earthly environment at first. I felt as if I knew my companion, the being from the spirit world who accompanied me like a long-time friend. However, this being who wore a white hooded robe was not anyone I have known on the Earth plane.

I said to my spirit friend, "Wow, this is a bad accident!" We were standing between the two totaled cars. Traffic was backed up on both sides of the street. Then I saw my car, and that's when I "remembered" my car accident. I saw a man wearing an orange-and-yellow coat looking into my car's driver's side. My spirit friend began to guide me back to my body. I remember wanting to come back to fulfill my purpose here on Earth. I also had the feeling that I would be back to the spirit realm very shortly because time is measured differently in that world. In other words, 80 years on Earth would be the same as one second on the Other Side. The spiritual realm is outside of, and is not limited by, time. All time is *now.*

As we started moving closer to my car and body, I abruptly stopped and said, "No!" I suddenly didn't want to go back. I looked over at the family that had collided with me. As soon as the question formed in my mind, "Are they okay?" the light being said, "Yes, they are all right; they are very upset with you, though." I saw all four people and their auras.

In the next second, I was back in my body. I saw the paramedic wearing the orange-and-yellow coat looking through the door at me. He asked me if I was okay. I said, "Yes, I was just walking in the street!" Later, just before I was placed in the ambulance, the paramedic asked me again, "Are you okay?" I then briefly told him about my experience, which I now know is called a near-death experience. I suppose paramedics hear about these encounters with the Other Side quite frequently when they come to the rescue of individuals who are near death.

From this experience, I know that in the spiritual realm we think and communicate in absolute truth. For example, if a person having a life review during an out-of-body or near-death experience sees an incident when they hurt another person's feelings, the person would not justify or make excuses for this wrong that was done. Instead, the individual would see it as an opportunity that was missed to be of service to another person. That's why I feel that it's so important to always hold the intention of practicing unconditional love in everything I do, and to never lose sight of it.

❦❦❦

Gentle Beings of Light
by Dorothy Womack

As my mother lay dying, she said that her room was filled with glowing beings. They were all smiling warmly, softly touching her skin and beckoning her to go with them. She was lifted up, and found herself walking in a beautiful, lush expanse of greenery. The place had fountains, flowers, and more glowing beings. The gardens were illuminated, but without sunlight. She wondered how she was able to walk, since she had been bedridden for four years.

These beings flew around her and lifted her up again, and she felt weightless. The glowing beings brought her back to her bed, kissed her cheek, and told her she'd be coming home soon. My mother said the glowing beings were so gentle and tender. Their eyes were large, filled with love, and their bodies were small and childlike. They had wings that felt like silk and shimmered like satin. They spoke to her in whispers and encouraged her to anticipate their imminent return. Mom said that no one should ever be afraid to die, and that we go to a beautiful place when we leave our bodies behind. Six weeks later, Mom died. Her courage in the face of certain death gave me the courage to face an uncertain life.

Into the Arms of Angels
by Jade D. Eisenhower

In 1998, my husband, Ike, was hospitalized and was considered terminally ill by his doctor. I remember overhearing the nurses saying on the evening before his death that they could not understand why he was still alive.

I, too, wondered how it could be possible for Ike to keep continuing on. I told Ike that it would be better for him to accept the hand of the Lord and walk in peace. I said, "Don't worry, the boys and I will be okay. You can watch over us from above and make a place for us. Please go. I'll be all right."

It was then that Ike took his last breath. As the color left his body, I saw a vaporized cloud of an image of my husband leaping up toward the ceiling. He reached out his hand and made contact with a hand that pulled him upward. I believe that it was the hand of an angel that was showing him the way.

Aunt Nina
by Sonia Huston

When I was 16, I died. It was the worst car accident in the history of the city of Vacaville, California. A police officer traveling at 65 miles per hour in a 30-mile-per-hour zone ran into the car I was riding in. She didn't have emergency lights or a siren on as she was responding to a silent burglar alarm across town. The exact moment she came over a steep hill, my three friends and I were making a U-turn at the crest of the hill. Right in the middle of our turn, she smashed into the back and the passenger side of the car. I was sitting in the passenger side. My two friends in the back of the car tragically died.

My injuries were severe and indeed quite life threatening. I lay in a coma and was on life support. The doctors told my family to expect the worst—that I probably wouldn't make it through the night.

While I was in my coma, my favorite aunt who had passed away six months prior to my accident came to me. She didn't say much, but she stood there with me while I took in the situation. Every time I turned to ask her something or cry to her, she merely smiled and nodded. I remember a glow around her, and the absolute peace that she brought to me during my state of panic. I wanted so badly to escape the confusion that filled me at that point. My first instinct was to just reach out and grab her hand and go off to wherever she had come from. She just smiled at me, reached her hand out to me, and nodded.

Then I was awake, beginning my long road to recovery. At first, the doctors assured my family that I would live as a vegetable. Then they said that I'd regain some of my old self but would never walk again. When I woke up, I couldn't speak, walk, or comprehend anything. I was an infant in a 16-year-old body. I worked through physical therapy, speech therapy, occupational therapy; and now I sit here and am writing this. I was left for dead, yet here I am promoting life.

Each time I feel that I can't go on in life, I go back to that moment when my Aunt Nina smiled and nodded at me. Yes, the old me died then, but the me I know now was born.

❤ ❤ ❤

PART II

*How <u>You</u> Can
See Angels, Too*

CHAPTER THIRTEEN

Healing Fears about Angel Visions

Each weekend, I give one- and two-day workshops called *Connecting with Your Angels* (this workshop is also available as a six-tape audio program of the same title from Hay House). Thousands of men, women, and children have taken this course, and the vast majority have been able to successfully connect with their angels. Many—probably half of my students—have seen angels during the workshop.

I've learned how to teach people how to see angels, both from my students' successes, as well as from the students who haven't been able to see. What I've learned is that *those who are willing and ready to see angels will see angels*. Now, when I say "angels," I am referring to those in heaven who help us and love us. So, whether you want to see your departed loved one, a grand archangel, Mother Mary, or a legion of beautiful angels, the process is the same.

You Are Clairvoyant—Right Now

The lens through which we see angels is an energy center located in the head between the two physical eyes. I call it "the third eye." Everyone has a third eye, and everyone's third eye is operating perfectly and continuously. I know this to be true because everyone has visual dreams—even when they can't remember them the next morning. Also, when people have near-death experiences (NDEs) they have visual experiences. They may see a movie of their life; angels and deceased loved ones; or a bright, brilliant light. In addition, hundreds of well-constructed scientific studies show that we all have an equal propensity for being accurate psychics. Many of these studies are described in my book *The Lightworker's Way*, published by Hay House.

So, *you can already see angels.* The question is, then, whether you *notice* them. A movie projector can be rolling in a theater, but if lens cap is covering it, the film won't be visible on the screen. Most people have lens caps covering their third eye, thus blocking awareness of their angel visions. These lens caps are put on by choice—consciously or unconsciously—and can also be removed by choice. In addition, you can control the level of your clairvoyance (meaning, your spiritual vision). Therefore, don't worry that once you open your third eye's window you'll be overwhelmed by seeing angels and deceased loved ones everywhere. Like a TV set, you can turn it up, down, on, or off at will. I personally choose to keep my third eye wide-open at all times because I love the beauty that I see. I've also lost my fears about seeing, which is the chief impediment to having angel visions.

Losing the Fear of Seeing

Let's go through some of the more common fears that cause people to choose to cover up their third eye. As you read each description, pay attention to your body's reactions. If you feel anything jump or tighten in your body, then you probably harbor that particular fear. If so, be sure to follow the guidance given for releasing the fear.

1. The fear of seeing frightening images. "Yes, I definitely want to see angels," my student Amy told me, "but only if I can first be 100 percent sure that I won't see any demons or gross-looking people."

Many people hold similar fears. While on the one hand, they strongly want to see the Divine beings of light; on the other hand, they fear that spiritual visions will open them up to perceiving frightening images.

The movie *The Sixth Sense* presented many realistic scenarios of what it's like to be a clairvoyant child. Until Cole, the child in the movie, understood his clairvoyance, he was frightened by it. But once he realized that the deceased people weren't chasing him, but simply wanted to talk to him, Cole appreciated his spiritual gift. The unrealistic part of *The Sixth Sense* and similar movies was its visual portrayal of deceased spirits. The movie showed them having blood, dismemberment, and gore on their bodies.

Nothing could be further from the truth! In fact, deceased people look better than most of us who are living! They appear to us visually in an "etheric body," which looks just like it did on the individual's best living days. Those who were emaciated, dismembered, or disabled are restored to wholeness, since that was their spiritual truth all along. They may appear to be the same age as when they passed, or a few years younger. When children pass away, they often grow up on the Other Side, so you may see them looking several years older than when you last saw them on the Earth plane.

Those on the Other Side don't have to deal with mundane matters such as bills, commuting, or arguing, so when you see your deceased loved one, you'll probably catch your breath in awe at his or her glowing attractiveness. Roughly 95 percent of deceased people whom I meet are happy, content, and well adjusted.

So, what about the other 5 percent? What if you're afraid that you'll meet an angry or vengeful deceased loved one or stranger? First of all, such people definitely do exist. And while they can exert some degree of influence on us—such as moving objects, turning on appliances, or whispering into our ears—they can't control or truly harm us.

Many people also fear the "fallen angels," beings of darkness and so-called evil. There is a breed of spirits that look like gargoyles, and they are the nearest thing to what you would call "fallen angels." These creatures have bony, leathery, batlike wings; squashed faces; and giant talons with claws. They also have no Divine light inside of them, which shows that they aren't God's creations, but instead, are thought-forms of fear that have been given a life force from the ego's belief in darkness and evil.

These Earthbound spirits and gargoyles don't bother the average person. In fact, they think most of us are pretty boring. Instead, they are attracted to people who abuse substances, who intentionally inflict psychological or physical pain onto others in business or personal relationships, and those who obsessively fear evil.

If your fear of these creatures keeps you from choosing to see God's Divine creations, let me ask you something: Would you rather walk down an alley with unsavory characters at noon or at midnight? The characters are there anyway, but personally, I'd rather *see* them so I could make the choice to walk on the other side of the street.

Spiritual sight reminds me of snorkeling in the tropics. You see glorious schools of the most beautiful fish imaginable, along with coral reefs and underwater foliage. But you might also see an occasional unattractive fish, including a sand shark. Does that keep you from snorkeling, or do you put your hands over your mask to avoid seeing unattractive sights and simultaneously block out the beauty of God's undersea world?

Here's some angel therapy for this fear, in whatever form it takes: Mentally ask Archangel Michael to stay next to you. Michael acts like a nightclub bouncer, ensuring that whoever comes into your orbit is someone from the Light. He also exudes a Divine energy that gives you courage in all situations. Michael, like all of the archangels, is able to be with everyone simultaneously who calls upon him and to respond individually to each of us. He is not limited by time or space restrictions, primarily because he doesn't believe in them. So when you call upon him, don't worry that you're pulling him away from a "more important" job.

The fear of seeing darkness or ghosts is the chief reason why people don't see angels or apparitions of their deceased loved ones. Fear, in any form, puts a lens cap over your third eye, much like putting your hands over your eyes during the frightening part of a movie. Second, your angels and deceased loved ones don't *want* to frighten you, so they won't appear to you as long as you're afraid of seeing them.

Ask Archangel Michael to help you release your fears. That is his Divine purpose, and his skill exceeds the most brilliant psychotherapist in helping us let go of negative emotions that block our spiritual sight. Mentally say:

> *"Archangel Michael, I ask that you enter into my mind, heart, and body. Please clean away all of the effects of mistakes in my thinking that keep me from enjoying clear spiritual sight. I am willing to release any fears that I have, knowing that you and God keep me eternally safe and protected. Please help give me the courage to see. Thank you."*

2. Fears left over from childhood. If you were a psychic child, you may have been punished or ridiculed. Maybe your parents told you that it was evil or crazy to see angels, deceased people, or the future. Perhaps you were called a know-it-all because you continually verbalized your accurate psychic insights. Or, it could be that the kids at school told you that you were weird because you talked about what you saw.

In some cases, children foresee a tragic event, such as a death, accident, or divorce. Children's viewpoint of cause-and-effect isn't yet matured, so some children mistakenly conclude that they "caused" the tragedy because they foresaw it.

All of these leftover fears from childhood are easier to eradicate from the head than from the heart. In other words, just because you know they are illogical does not remove the emotional pangs that you may feel whenever you think about reopening your psychic sight.

These childhood-related fears are so similar to another group of fears, described in point 3 below, that the angel therapy prescription for them is the same.

3. Fear of breaking a "rule" and incurring God's wrath or going to hell. As much as you want to speak to dear departed Mom, your Christian roots might scream at you unconsciously that "it's a sin to talk to dead people! After all, that's what the Bible says!" In fact, the Bible *does* warn against talking to mediums and wizards, but it is also filled with accounts of people communicating with angels and the dead. Jesus himself talks to the dead as he is reviving them.

I think we can all agree that much of the Bible is open to personal interpretation. My own take on the Bible's warnings is that we shouldn't turn our lives over to the dead. In other words, you shouldn't pray to your dead relatives to give you all of your guidance and advice.

Just because people die, they don't automatically become saints (unless they were saintly while they were living). The dead don't instantly know how to access all of the universal wisdom. So, your reasons for seeing or talking to deceased loved ones are basic ones—to keep your relationship going, to tell them you love them, or to heal an old wound—not to turn that person into your spiritual guru.

I also feel the wisdom of Apostle Paul's words when he said that we all have the spiritual gift of prophecy, and that we should aspire to use this gift as long as it is used with love.[1]

Angel therapy cure: forgiveness of those who gave us the rules, or those involved with our scary childhood prophecies.

4. The fear of going crazy, dying, ascending, or losing control (including becoming irresponsible) if you become clairvoyant. Many of my students tell me that they would very much *like* to open their third eye and be clairvoyant. However, they simultaneously fear that in doing so, they'd also lose touch with reality. They fear becoming a blithering idiot, a spacy weirdo, or a person devoid of personality. A similar fear is voiced by people who worry that if they really delved into enlightenment and intuition, they'd lose their ability to tolerate their job, their marriage, and their life in general. They fear that they'd become impulsive and suddenly quit their job, file for divorce, and move to a tropical island. In the same vein is the fear that if they really opened up to the Divine, they'd ascend or complete their purpose before they're ready to leave the earth. In other words, they would die.

But it's the lower-self—the ego—that dies, goes crazy, and loses control when you open up your true self's spiritual gifts. Opening up your psychic senses involves losing your fears, your unforgiveness, and your judgments. When you lose your fears, your ego loses its power base. And if you became completely serene, the ego would have no voice, no life at all. So fears in this category all stem from "ego identification," or believing that you are your ego.

When you open up to the Divine, you become more loving and centered. Impulsive behavior comes from the ego, not from the true self. You may become guided to make life changes, and you may in fact end up quitting your job, divorcing, or moving. But when these changes are guided by your true self, they are done with love and harmony. God and the angels would never ask you to make a life change in a way that is hurtful to yourself or others. If life changes are necessary for your spiritual growth and life purpose, you will receive step-by-step assistance that will smooth your path, as well as the path of your family members. God's guidance comes with angels' wings.

The fear of dying in response to awakened psychic abilities can also stem from past-life issues. If you are a "lightworker" in this life—a person who feels compelled to help people and the world through spiritual means—you have probably been a light-worker in past lives. Even if you're not sure whether you believe in past lives or not, you may find physical and emotional benefits from going through a past-life regression to clear these fears.

Approximately 55 percent of my students have found, during a past-life regression, that they were killed or hurt during past lives in which they had psychic abilities. During the Inquisition and witch hunt eras, people who were mystics, spiritual healers, prophets, or just "different" were persecuted and executed by governments and organized religions. Such people were hanged, burned at the stake, tortured, or had their loved ones and possessions taken from them.

If you have had such a past-life experience, you may have deep-seated fears about reopening your psychic gifts. This is especially true among people who report having *no* clairvoyant or visual abilities in this life. Their third eye is tightly capped, as they cling to life to avoid going through a fate similar to that of past times. The irony is, though, that in our current culture, it is more safe to be psychic than to be closed off. Psychic and intuitive abilities provide a road map that helps you find right livelihood, appropriate relationships, and healthful lifestyles. Those who are closed off often succumb to claustrophobic or abusive situations, which can endanger mental and physical health.

If you believe that your psychic abilities may have been the reason why you were killed or hurt in a past life, here are some powerful remedies. First, say these affirmations repeatedly:

It is safe for me to be psychic.
It is safe for me to see my truth.
It is safe for me to see the future.
I am safe now, expressing my true self.

Also, I highly recommend going through a past-life regression, with the intention of uncovering the past life related to your suppressed clairvoyance. Most hypnotherapists are qualified to take you through a past-life regression. Audios, including my *Past-Life Regression with the Angels* and *Karma Releasing* audio programs (published by Hay House), can guide you through the process. You can also ask your unconscious mind to release all relevant information about your underlying reasons for choosing to cap your third eye. Say aloud or affirm mentally in your unconscious mind:

> *"Unconscious mind and higher self, I ask you to reveal to me the reasons why I have chosen to close my clairvoyance. Please help me understand what happened to me in this life or a past one, related to my clairvoyance. Please help me release embedded fears, and help me open up my window of clairvoyance so that I may once again see truth and beauty. Thank you."*

Your unconscious mind won't allow you to remember or reexperience anything that you can't handle. The memories will come to you in waves at various times, as opposed to a flood of continual memories. You may see them in your dreams, or simply feel a huge surge of emotions or physical sensations when watching a historical movie. Or, it could come to you as a knowingness, where you just feel that you were burned at the stake in Eastern Europe, for instance. You could suddenly understand that your aversion to turtleneck sweaters stems from that past life in which you were hung. In my personal and clinical experience, I've found that past-life regressions allow us to clear ourselves on the deepest level through the process of "catharsis," or letting go.

Other past-life scenarios correlated with closed psychic abilities include those who witnessed the crucifixion, and decided that it was so horrible that they never wanted to see anything again. In addition, those who lived during bloody battles, especially the

Native American wars, have created lasting traumas that make them afraid to "see" in their present life.

Finally, unconscious beliefs can cause us to choose closed clairvoyance. For example, one elderly woman in my weekend psychic development class kept telling me, "I just want to see an angel before I die! That's all I want!" It occurred to me that she definitely would see angels when she died, but she insisted on seeing an angel beforehand.

During the first day of the workshop, she was totally frustrated because she couldn't see anything. She kept comparing herself to the other students who successfully saw angels, auras, deceased loved ones, and psychic images in the class exercises. By the second day, we were all rooting for her, praying that she would get her wish. But the second day proved just as fruitless for her.

Then, during the last psychic development exercise on the last day of class, she had her breakthrough. I heard her excitedly scream, "I saw! I saw!" Her timing was interesting. Why had she waited until the class was nearly over before allowing herself to see? It turned out that her unconscious mind had taken her wish literally. She kept affirming, "I want to see an angel before I die," and so her underlying fear was, "If I see an angel, then I will die."

5. The fear of losing someone's love or approval if you open your clairvoyance. If your family members or spouse come from a fundamental religious background, or if they are skeptical about all things esoteric, you might worry about their reactions if you suddenly reported seeing angels.

The angels will guide you in all of your relationships, and they would never ask you to say or do anything that would spark a conflict. They will give you clear help as to what to say, to whom, and when to say it. If you surrender your fear to God, He will ensure that you can "come out of the spiritual closet" in a harmonious way.

From an Earthly standpoint, relationships are only satisfying if we allow our authentic self to be known. Otherwise, how can you feel truly loved? As long as you're hiding who you really are in a relationship, you'll believe that your partner is in love with the phony self that you're pretending to be.

In committed love relationships, it is essential that you tell your partner what's going on with you. Admit your confusion, doubts, and your own skepticism, as well as your desires and dreams. Realize that your skeptical or fundamentalist partner may react initially out of his or her own fears. Try to gently help your partner with his or her fears, instead of becoming automatically defensive if your partner isn't immediately in love with the idea that you see and hear angels. Seek an Earth angel in the form of an open-minded marriage counselor to help you work through any signs that you have a "spiritually unbalanced relationship."

6. Fear of what the angel might say if you saw one. Fears in this category include worrying that your deceased loved one is angry with you for something that you did, or did not do. It also includes fears that your deceased loved one disapproves of your current lifestyle. People are constantly asking me for mediumship sessions because they worry that their deceased loved one is angry that they weren't with them when the last breath was taken, because of the decision to take them off life-support systems; or because the living person got a divorce.

Ninety percent of the deceased people whom I meet are quite the opposite of angry. They are, in fact, some of the most serene people I've ever met! The other 10 percent or so fall into two categories: those who were chronic worriers before death and who continue to be after death, and those who are racked with remorse over the way they lived their lives. Statistically, the chances are extremely high that your deceased loved ones are peaceful and happy.

However, if they're unhappy, it's highly unlikely that *you* are the reason. I've never, ever had a deceased loved one say that they were unhappy about being taken off of life support, or angry that a living relative wasn't at their funeral or deathbed. In fact, those who are murdered rarely even tell me that they're vengeful toward their assailants.

The deceased receive nearly 'round-the-clock "mental health" care from the moment they arrive in heaven. Most of this care is focused on helping the newly deceased let go of emotional baggage such as anger, judgments and unforgiveness. Those who are new to heaven are urged to view themselves and everyone else with compassion, knowing that everyone's doing the best that they know how.

If your deceased loved one was a chronic worrier during life, then chances are that this person may still be fretting in heaven (one more reason to heal this life-robbing personality trait while you're living!). In such cases, your most loving and helpful solution is to pray for your deceased loved one's peace of mind. Ask God to send extra angels to him or her. Mentally tell your deceased loved one that worry is unnecessary and doesn't help anyone or any situation. Or, write a letter to your deceased loved one, and write down any responses that you receive as thoughts, words, feelings, or visions. Through letter writing, you can heal any unresolved issues and develop an even closer relationship than you both shared on Earth.

7. Fear that you won't be able to see the angels. A sad paradox is that those who want to see the angels the most are often those who are the least likely to see them! The reason is that they are trying too hard. The underlying fearful belief is: "Maybe I won't be able to see the angel," and this negative thought creates a self-fulfilling prophecy.

Straining to do *anything*, whether it's playing tennis, creating a love relationship, or conceiving a baby, rarely yields positive results. Our muscles get tense, our creative thoughts flee, and we begin holding our breath.

In the following chapters, I'll be describing specific methods to help you see angels. However, the initial underlying attitude needs to be one of positive expectation. The angels say that "our intentions create our experiences." In this case, that means that your intention to see an angel will create the experience of seeing one. But an underlying negative intention such as, "Gee, I hope that I'll really be able to do this," will create a negative expectation and hurt your chances of seeing an angel.

Any activities that you can undertake in order to quell nervous tension and excitement, such as yoga, massage, deep breathing, quiet meditation, or a walk outside in nature will increase the frequency and intensity of your angel visions.

$$\text{3€ 3€ 3€}$$

CHAPTER FOURTEEN

A One-Week Plan to Open Yourself to Angel Visions

This chapter outlines a powerful plan of action that can give you the maximum opportunity to see angels. For some of you, the results will be immediate, and you may see angels or your deceased loved one right away. Others may need to be more patient, and it could be several weeks before you have angel visions. However, if you follow these steps, you'll definitely have breakthroughs that will lead you toward sightings. I'm asking you to perform these steps every day for seven days. As soon as you're ready to see angels, they will appear.

You probably noticed that a common thread among the stories of people who saw their deceased loved one in a dream or as an apparition was that the person was in a state of crisis, or had a strong emotional need to connect with their loved one. When you deeply long for certain individuals, a signal is emitted to heaven. Those above know that you strongly desire a conversation with your deceased loved one. In fact, your loved one has probably already visited you. If you "felt" his or her presence, you were most likely correct. You didn't see the person or you don't remember your dream interactions because of your heightened emotional state of grief, fear, or anger.

If you've been afraid to see an apparition, your deceased loved one won't appear to you because he or she loves you and doesn't want to scare you. However, if you've honestly faced your fears, such as those outlined in the previous chapter, and taken spiritual or psychological steps to heal those fears, your deceased loved one is more likely to appear to you now.

There is never a guarantee that the person will appear to you, and if you don't see him or her, it's important not to let yourself get upset. It doesn't mean that your deceased loved one is mad at you or that they don't love you just because you haven't seen him or her. If someone else in your family has seen your deceased loved one, it's not a sign of favoritism—it just means that the other person was more "ready" to see an apparition than you were.

It takes a lot of energy for a person in the spirit world to appear in apparition form, similar to how it feels when we dive to the deepest ocean floor. Sometimes deceased loved ones have to "borrow" a charge from the "battery" of their own spirit guides to have enough energy to glow visibly for the living. One study of individuals who had seen apparitions from their deathbed found that the vast majority only saw their deceased loved one's apparition for five minutes or less.[1] The spirit world can often only sustain an apparition appearance for brief periods of time. So, I don't want you to expect to spend hours and hours conversing with your deceased loved one. Some people do, but usually you'll see and talk to the person from the spirit world rather briefly. Yet even though it's a short visit, you'll likely find it life-changing and highly therapeutic.

Your visit with a guardian angel of the winged variety, or with a spirit guide who glows so bright that you may not even see his or her facial features, might also be brief. In such encounters, though, you'll have a feeling of time standing still. So afterward, it may be difficult for you to calculate how much time your angel encounter involved.

Seven-Day Plan for Having an Angel Vision

Here are the steps that I teach the students in my mediumship, psychic development, and clairvoyance classes. Usually I suggest that you try one or two of these steps at a time, but I understand that you're very serious about seeing an angel or a deceased loved one, so I'm going to ask you to go into heavy-duty training, and perform all of the steps in sequence. Just keep going through the days until you have your breakthrough vision.

As I said earlier, it might happen on day 2 or day 42. But one thing's for sure: If you follow these steps as prescribed, you will eventually have visions. Your determination in following the steps is up to you. If this process is truly important to you, then please perform these steps for as long as necessary. As an added benefit, you may also find that these steps may help you feel lighter, happier, stronger, and healthier.

First, choose a day to begin, and write it on your calendar as "The Beginning of Angel Visions." The day before you're scheduled to begin, you'll need to stock up on some Earthly supplies and shop for foods that will enhance your psychic abilities. Go to a health food store, if possible, for these items. Or, find a local fruit stand or a grocery store with superior produce.

Buy yourself several types of fresh fruit, preferably organic. In chronological order of their ability to support your psychic abilities, purchase: fresh pineapple, grapefruit, oranges, apples, lemons, berries, and melons. Then, purchase some organic, whole-grain breakfast cereal; whole-grain rice; mixed salad greens; natural salad dressing (without chemical ingredients); raw nuts; hummus; and some meat replacements such as tofu, seitan, Veat brand meat substitute, Chiken brand meat substitute, or vegi-burgers. Or, look through your health food store's deli and frozen food section for various meat substitutes. While you're at it, buy one or two vegetarian cookbooks, or *Vegetarian Times* magazine, to guide you through the ins and outs of a vegetarian diet.

Maintaining a vegetarian diet is the quickest route to developing clairvoyance. Even quicker is a "vegan" diet, which means that you avoid all meat, fowl, fish, or dairy products, and use meat substitutes and soy milk products. In fact, dairy products, red meat, chocolate, and alcohol are the greatest blocks to clairvoyance. For further explanation on the link between diet and psychic abilities, please see my books *Chakra Clearing* and *Divine Prescriptions*.

Note: Each day's morning activities will take at least 20 minutes, so you may need to adjust your normal morning routine and set your alarm clock 20 minutes earlier than normal. Some of the activities may seem odd to you, and you may wonder if you could skip some of them. My advice to you is to perform these activities, and if you feel uncomfortable about any of them, ask God and your angels to help ease your discomfort or give you a substitute activity. The first day, you may feel overwhelmed by all that I'm asking you to do, but you'll soon develop a routine that will take less effort. Besides, any extra effort will be worth it, and you'll find that you have more energy throughout the day as a result.

What to Do Each Day

1. Morning meditation. Immediately after waking up and having your morning bathroom break, meditate before engaging in any lengthy conversation with family members or roommates. Each day, there's a different morning and evening meditation to focus upon. You can combine this meditation with your other normal meditation practices, or use it solo.

2. Journal. Next, write (on a notepad or in a formal journal or diary) a letter to whomever you want to see. It could be a carte blanche letter to "Whoever is my guardian angel," to a specific deceased loved one, to Jesus or a saint, or to God asking to see whom you're supposed to see. Your letter needs to be from your heart, where you pour out your feelings. Remember that all of the stories in this book showed the correlation between a person having strong feelings, and then later seeing a deceased loved one or angels. So, let your feelings out in your letter! Don't worry about grammar, spelling, or proper syntax. Just write from the heart.

3. Chant. In this next step (and you may need to go outside to do the following two steps), you will use the ancient science called "toning" to open up your third eye. Chant the sound of God or Creation seven times, preferably out loud. If your family is skeptical, you can chant quietly, but in general, the louder the better. If you have reservations about chanting, or fears that this may be a spooky occult practice, please read the section at the end of this chapter entitled "About Chanting." You'll read one woman's remarkable story of having an angel vision after she began this practice.

Close your eyes and say "Aaaahhhh, Uuuuhhhh, Mmmm," seven times. While you're chanting, place your focus on the area between your two physical eyes, and hold the positive thought, "It is safe for me to see angels." Concentrate on seeing whoever it is you want to see. If you have any negative or frightening thoughts, please don't fight them. Instead, mentally ask your angels to take the thoughts away.

4. Spin. After you have chanted the AUM sound seven times, stand up and spread your arms straight out from your sides. With your eyes open, find an item or a shape in the wall, a nearby tree, a curtain, or some other interesting eye-level object. This is your "visual anchor." Then look at that object and slowly spin your body to the right (clockwise). Your body will get to an angle where you can no longer see your visual anchor. Just keep spinning clockwise, and turn your head to the left to spot your visual anchor again, and guide your body back to face the visual anchor.

Do this spinning exercise three times each morning. If you feel dizzy, it means that your third-eye chakra (the window of clairvoyance) is dirty. As you cleanse your chakra through meditation, chanting, light eating, and spinning, you'll be able to rotate more times without feeling dizzy. For now, though, spin slowly during each rotation. You can also stop at the end of the three spins and put your hands in a prayer position (or "Namaste" position) in front of your chest as a way to stop the dizziness.

5. Eat in the light. You should eat a vegetarian or vegan diet (no meat or dairy) to the extent that you want to have angel visions. In other words, the more vegetarian foods that you can eat, the more readily your angel visions will come. So, a 70 percent vegetarian diet would yield a 70 percent chance of seeing an angel or deceased loved one, and so on.

In addition, mentally ask your angels to heal any cravings you may have for the two substances that block psychic abilities the most: alcohol and chocolate. If you're really serious and sincere about seeing angels, you'll abstain from these two products for now. The angels can release you from *desiring* alcohol or chocolate so that you won't feel deprived. Just ask for their help by saying something such as:

> *"Angels, I want to see you, so I ask you to enter my body, mind, and heart, and heal away any fears or sense of emptiness that leads me to crave mood-altering food or drinks. I am willing to release the need to eat chocolate or drink alcohol. I know that these substances are poor substitutes for Divine love and energy. Thank you, and Amen."*

In addition, keep your caffeine, sugar, nicotine, and processed food intake to a minimum during your seven-day process. Instead, drink plenty of room-temperature spring or artesian water (not sparkling, purified, distilled, or drinking water); or rainwater that you catch in bowls during a rainstorm. Or, drink freshly squeezed citrus juice, especially if it comes from organic produce. You'll find that natural water and fresh, organic juices boost your energy much more than any caffeinated beverage.

6. Nature time. Five minutes a day, take off your shoes, socks, or nylons, and stand with your bare feet on Mother Earth. Let your flesh connect with soil, grass, or sand. You and the earth need to touch each other in a "mystical meeting" to psychically exchange vital information—as well as playful love—with one another. By keeping this Divine daily appointment with your Mother, you will feel more of a kinship with all of life. And part of opening your psychic visions is knowing that you are one with everyone and everything.

In addition, make sure that you're surrounded by healthy, live plants in your home and office. Plants absorb the energy of our fear and stress in the same way that they absorb carbon dioxide. It is especially important to sleep next to a live plant. The broad-leafed varieties, such as pothos or philodendrons, are especially adept at absorbing negative energy.

7. Exercise. Every day, engage in some sort of heart-opening physical activity, such as yoga, brisk walking, running, swimming, pedaling, or any other exercise that elevates your pulse for at least 30 minutes. Aerobic exercise clears away fear's toxic residue, which builds up in the body.

8. Evening chant. Chant "Aum" seven times, as discussed in Step 3.

9. Evening meditation. Spend at least ten minutes alone, even if you have to lock yourself in the bathroom, and take several deep breaths. Focus on the evening meditation corresponding to the particular day of your Seven-Day Plan.

10. Evening angel discussion. As you fall asleep, mentally talk to your angel or deceased loved one. Pour your heart out about your feelings, about what happened to you during the day, and any issue that you need assistance with. Ask your angel or deceased loved one to enter your dreams or to visibly appear to you. Ask for help in losing your fears so that you can stay calm and centered. Ask for help, also, to remember any dream encounter that you may have with your angel or deceased loved one (although most dream encounters are so vivid that they are unforgettable).

Morning and Evening Meditations

Day 1—Morning: *"I now feel myself surrounded by the healing presence of my angels. I feel their wings enfolding me, helping me to know that I am safe and eternally loved. As I breathe in and out, I feel their unconditional love for me as warmth in my chest and heart. I allow myself to feel loved, knowing that it is safe to open my heart to Divine love."*

Day 1—Evening: *"I know that I am safe, continuously guarded by large angels who watch over me. I know that God's infinite wisdom and unconditional love are supporting me right now. I ask for* [whoever it is you would like to see] *to appear to me visually. I would like to see* [name of whoever you would like to see]. *I know that it is safe for me to see. I don't strain or push, but I now allow visions to come to me at a pace that I can easily handle."*

❦❦❦

Day 2—Morning: *"Everything is in Divine and perfect order, right now. I see angels in God's perfect timing, and I release any need to rush my angel visions. As I breathe in and out, I release* *any old toxins in my body related to fears about opening myself up to psychic visions. I release toxins related to any past experience that was painful. [Breathe in and out deeply.] I let everything go. I now see a golden light inside my head. I see that golden light forming a rope, and I feel that rope moving from the inside my head, out into the room, like a pipe cleaner. I now feel my third eye being cleansed by the light of my Holy Spirit. I allow Spirit to cleanse and open me to Divine experiences, now."*

Day 2—Evening: *"I breathe in deeply, drawing in the life force energy of the world. I am one with this energy. My angels and deceased loved ones are one with this energy. As I exhale completely, I breathe out all stress, doubt, and fear completely. I now breathe in deeply, drawing in faith, confidence, and knowingness. I exhale skepticism. I inhale acceptance. I exhale fear. I inhale faith. I exhale everything that I do not want in my life. I inhale everything that I desire. I exhale anger. I inhale gratitude."*

⚜⚜⚜

Day 3—Morning: *"Dear God and Holy Spirit, I deeply desire to see my angel* [or name of deceased loved one]. *I ask Your help in bringing this about. Please give me clear Divine guidance that I will easily understand to help me know what to do in order to have an angel vision. Please help me lose any fears that may be blocking my spiritual sight. Please help me see Your miraculous angels."*

Day 3—Evening: *"I now ask my angels and* [name of deceased loved one and/or ascended master whom you would like to see] *to enter my dreams. My heart and mind are open to all possibilities, and I am ready to receive love and truth. I know that I am safe in having angel visions, and I affirm that Divine love encircles me now. It is safe for me to see angels. It is safe* *for me to see truth. It is safe for me to see the future. It is safe for me to see."*

❦❦❦

Day 4—Morning: *"My spiritual sight is now wide open, and all around me is incredible beauty. Everywhere I look, I see evidence of love. I see loving actions, the exquisiteness of nature, and the attractiveness of everyone and everything. As I see only love, then only love can come into my awareness. I now see love in the embodiment of angels."*

Day 4—Evening: *"I ask for Archangel Michael to enter my dreams tonight and clear away any fears that could be keeping me from having full faith. I now allow God's Divine love to expand throughout my being, filling me with eternal confidence and eradicating any illusions of fear. I am safe, and I am loved."*

❦❦❦

Day 5—Morning: *"Today I see the glowing lights of angels that constantly surround every person. I see glowing shades of white, gold, green, blue, and purple around everyone's head and shoulders. I easily connect with this angel energy, and I receive Divine messages throughout the day. These messages always speak of Divine love and selfless service, and help me stay centered in an awareness of my gratitude for heaven upon earth."*

Day 5—Evening: *"I allow goodness to come to me without forcing or chasing anything. I know that forcing anything to happen comes from an underlying thought of fear. I know that fear blocks the very experiences I desire. I completely surrender my desire to have an angel vision. I trust God and heaven to bring* *my heart's desire to me. My only task is to open the door, by surrendering all forms of fear. The rest will happen naturally."*

❀❀❀

Day 6—Morning: *"Today I intend to have a happy day. I ask God and my angels to guide me so that I may feel happiness throughout the day. I ask to bring blessings to everyone who sees, meets, or thinks of me today. I ask to be an earth angel today."*

Day 6—Evening: *"Dear* [angel or name of the being whom you would like to see], *I deeply desire to see you. Please enter my dreams, or manifest into a visible apparition so that I may see and experience you without delay. I ask that you allow me to see you. If I am blocking this experience in any way, please give me a strong and clear message so that I may have clear spiritual sight."*

❀❀❀

Day 7—Morning: *"As I tune in to my third eye, I am aware of sparkling white, blue, and purple light.* [Please take a moment to close your physical eyes and see these colors right in front of you.] *I now ask for Archangel Raphael to place his index finger on my third eye, and heal away any last remaining vestiges of fear that may be covering my spiritual vision. I trust that my veil has lifted and that I now can see clearly. I am ready to see now!"*

Day 7—Evening: *"I am now aware of the presence of my guardian angels. As I breathe in and out, I relax and attune to the awareness of them. I allow myself to feel the depth of their love for me. I feel their warmth. I feel their unconditional love. I am*

one with my angels. I am one with love. I now give myself per-
mission to visually connect with my angels."

About Chanting

To some, the idea of chanting may seem unnatural or uncomfortable, yet it is an ancient practice for achieving spiritual visions.
Far from being an occult practice, chanting stems from affirming
the holy name of our Creator. When chanting the word *Aum,* you
are actually singing a love song to God. *Aum* is actually the root
of the word *Amen,* which closes most Christian prayers.

Here is a story of a woman who was able to have an angel
vision, thanks to the help that chanting gave her.

How Chanting Helped Me See My Angel
by Molly Donohue

On Christmas day of 1999, I saw an angel floating above my
bed. While I was reading Doreen's book *Divine Guidance*, I said
a prayer that I would like to actually see one of my angels. I had
been following Doreen's advice about chanting "Ahhhh,
"Uuuuhhhh," Mmmmm" seven times every morning and every
night for about a week.

In the middle of the night, I was woken up by the sight of a
bright reddish-white light. The sight was strange, as if there was
a planetarium above my bed. The brilliance of the light dimmed
somewhat, and I saw a beautiful female angel lying on her side,
looking down at me.

Of course I was startled, but soon after, I was filled with a
feeling of warmth and love, and I simply wasn't scared anymore.
I remembered reading in Doreen's book that angels are messengers, so I asked what her name was and what message she had
for me.

Telepathically, she said that her name was Annabelle. She looked just like the angels in Renaissance paintings, and her message was simple. She wanted me to know that I was supremely loved, more than I can even imagine. She wanted me to know that I was watched over every moment, and a legion of angels and guides waited for my requests. I asked her about a book I thought I was supposed to write. She confirmed that it was Divine guidance for me to write the book, but that was not her role.

She was sent in answer to a prayer, and to express love—Divine love. I basked in the love and radiance for at least 30 minutes. I even went to the bathroom during that time, and she was still there when I came back out, just radiating love and light. Then she slowly faded out, back to just reddish white, then to nothingness. It was one of the most wonderful experiences of my life. I now continue to see, hear, and feel my angels all the time.

)€)€)€

CHAPTER FIFTEEN

How to See an Angel

I f you follow the Seven-Day Plan from Chapter 14, continue repeating the procedures for as many days as it takes, and if you're truly ready to see an angel, there's no reason why you won't have an angel vision. The methods outlined in the previous chapter are all-powerful, time-honored steps that lead to visions. They work . . . if you commit to practicing them consistently.

As you've read in the stories in the first half of this book, different people have different ways of seeing their angels. Yet, whether their experience involved a dream, a waking state, seeing lights, or having a helpful encounter with a mysterious stranger, the authors of the stories you've read about have one thing in common: Their angel vision was deeply meaningful and life-changing.

You probably have a preference regarding the way you'd like to see your angels (and in this chapter, I'm using the word *angel* to collectively mean an angel with wings, a deceased loved one, or an ascended master); yet your angel vision will occur exactly in the manner that you're most ready for. If you would be frightened by seeing a big beautiful angel in your living room, then your angel vision will occur as a dream or by seeing lights.

In my *Connecting with Your Angels* workshop, I find that my audience members experience angel visions in many different ways, including seeing an angel:

- with their physical eyes open;
- in their mind's eye, with their physical eyes shut; and
- as a partial picture in their mind's eye.

Some of my audience members experience angel visions that look like wispy, smokelike images. Others see angels that are more opaque and solid looking. Some people see angels in their mind's eye that look like they are stationed over other people. To others, the angels that they see in their mind's eye seem to be located inside their own head.

When I see angels, I typically have my eyes open. When I was a child, I saw deceased people as opaque and solid looking. I couldn't distinguish them from living people. Now that I'm older, my angel visions are less opaque. The angels that I see remind me of the experience of being in a living room with friends, with the TV set on. I can see both the people who are physically present with me, as well as the people on the set. I know that those who are on TV are not as "real" as those who are sitting on the sofa next to me.

So, your angel visions will probably have a different quality from seeing a living person. Nonetheless, you will know that you are interacting with a sentient being who is quite alive. You won't have much doubt, if any, whether your experience is real. In most angel visions, you'll receive a message from the angel that will be wordlessly transferred into your heart or your mind. You'll "know" or "feel" exactly what the angel is telling you.

Please Don't Strain!

You'll block your angel visions if you try too hard.

Do pray hard to see your angel and to release your fears that could block angel visions.

Please don't force the experience to happen.

Let the angel visions come to you.

Imagine that you are a satellite dish that receives signals.

Different Ways to See Angels

After following the Seven-Day Plan, and repeating it if necessary, you'll probably have a spontaneous angel vision. Most likely, it will happen when you least expect it. For instance, you'll awaken in the middle of the night and see an angel standing near the foot of the bed. The incredible love permeating from the angel will allay any fears that you'd normally have. Or, you'll be driving and spontaneously see an angel hovering over the hood of your car. The possibilities for your out-of-the-blue angel vision are endless, and I hope that you'll write and tell me about your experience (the address is in the "About the Author" section at the end of this book).

In addition to a spontaneous angel vision, here are some exercises that can also promote your visual encounter with a heavenly being. Practicing an exercise is different from forcing one to occur, as long as you don't have a sense of strain while you're conducting it. You'll have the best success with these exercises if you do them on an empty or nearly empty stomach, and without the influence of any caffeine, sugar, nicotine, alcohol, or other mood-altering substances.

While conducting these exercises, it's vital to hold positive expectations that you will see angels! The angels always say, "Your intentions create your experiences." So, if you're holding negative intentions toward angel visions such as, "Gee, I hope I can really do this," or "I'm kind of doubtful that I'm qualified to see angels," you'll be blocked because you *expect* to be blocked.

Doubts are normal from time to time. The key is to be aware of these negative intentions, and then to mentally ask your angels to help remove these thoughts, feelings and their residue. Before you begin these exercises, take a few moments to close your eyes, breathe deeply, and see or feel eight glass globes stacked on top of each other. From top to bottom, the colors of the globes are:

- Purple
- Violet-red
- Deep blue
- Light blue
- Emerald green
- Yellow
- Orange
- Red

See or feel these globes as brightly colored, and free of any spots or dirt. Picture a bright white light illuminating the interior of each globe.

Then mentally affirm:

I now easily see the spiritual world.
I am a powerful clairvoyant who uses my gift in
beautiful service to the world.
It is safe for me to see.
I am surrounded by safety, protection, and quiet
peacefulness.

Partner Exercises

In each partner exercise, you'll want to work with someone who is open-minded and who believes in angels (or who would like to believe in angels). Although it is very possible to gain important angelic experiences while working with skeptics, their negative mind-set toward life-after-death and angels could frustrate you in your initial attempts at seeing angels. So, please select your most faith-filled friend or family member.

Wall work—Ask your friend to stand against a plain white wall. The wall should have a minimum of texture and no wallpaper. A solid white screen, used for movie projection, works wonderfully well, also.

Ask your friend to close her eyes so that you don't feel any sense of pressure or awkwardness as you conduct this exercise. Then, take a few deep breaths, and squint your eyes slightly. Soften your gaze, as if you're looking past your friend.

With your softened focus, scan around your friend's head and shoulders. Don't strain to see anything; let the visual awareness come to you naturally. Notice if you see or sense any white light, or other colors glowing around your friend. Perhaps you see waves of energy, similar to seeing heat waves emanating from the street on a hot day.

Then, take another deep breath and close your eyes. Compare what you see around your friend's head and shoulders once you close your eyes (some people see the spirit world more easily if they shut their eyes). If you "see" easier with your physical eyes closed, then please keep them shut throughout the rest of this exercise. However, you may see the energy or light of the angels easier with your eyes open, and if so, please keep your physical eyes open during the exercise.

Once you see any sort of light, bump, or other indication of a presence, keep breathing in and out as your spiritual sight adjusts to seeing. Just like when you exit a dark movie theater during the day, your eyes will need some time to adjust and focus on what they are seeing. Don't worry whether this is your imagination or not; just keep noticing any details about the angels around your partner.

Pairing work—This is an exercise designed so that both partners can simultaneously have an angel vision. First, sit facing your friend. Hold hands, and both of you should have your eyes closed. Rest your hands in a comfortable place, such as one person's lap, so that your hands don't get tired. Breathe in and out regularly, as we sometimes hold our breath when we're under pressure. Breathing opens up the psychic senses. Also, take your time with this exercise, since any sense of time urgency could block you.

Now, imagine what it would be like if you could see your partner's guardian angels. Just give yourself permission to imagine seeing your friend's angels. It doesn't matter whether you're making this up or really seeing those angels. Just let yourself see them.

What do they look like? Are they tall or short? Do they seem female, male, or androgynous? What color are their eyes? What is the style and color of their hair? Do you see any wings? Any other details about them? Do you have a sense of any message that the angels are sending your partner?

After a few minutes of seeing the angels around your partner, go ahead and tell your partner everything that you saw, felt, heard, or thought. Don't worry whether it was "real" or not. One of the reasons why children are so highly psychic is that they are unconcerned with differentiating between mere imagination and true reality. Our guardedness as adults is one of the chief blocks that keeps us from seeing beyond the veil. The irony is that, when you let down any defensiveness against mistaking fantasy for reality, you'll have your real angel vision breakthroughs.

You will know or feel the reality of your vision, and your partner will validate that the vision rings true for him or her. However, if you doubt whether you really saw an angel, be sure to ask God and the angels to guide you to a real angel vision, or to help you release any erroneous doubts that keep you from enjoying your angel visions.

There is no limit to the number of times you can see your winged guardian angels; or someone such as Jesus, Yogananda, or a saint. However, your recently deceased loved one may not be able to visually appear to you frequently. It takes a tremendous amount of energy for a deceased person to appear in apparition form, so you may only see your deceased loved one once a month, for instance. After all, newly deceased people can't stay on the Earth-plane level continuously. They've got heavenly growth work to do before they can be assigned as someone's permanent spirit guide. But after tuning into him or her visually, you will be able to sense and feel their presence more readily. And be assured that your deceased loved one always hears your prayers, messages, requests, and questions. They are never out of earshot, and when you call upon them, they are with you as soon as they possibly can be.

Solo Exercises

Appointment with an angel—Decide which heavenly being you would like to see. It could be a deceased loved one or your winged guardian angel, for example. Then, get out your calendar and choose a day and time when you'll have at least two uninterrupted hours alone. Mark on your calendar, "My appointment with an angel."

Then, go somewhere alone, such as the bathroom, the out-
doors, or your meditation area. Close your physical eyes and focus
on the heavenly being you would like to see. Mentally call to this
being. Send the being love energy from your heart and belly.

Then, mentally explain to the being that you would like to
meet with him or her (give the exact day and time of your appointment). If you get a strong feeling that this is not a good day or
time for your angel or deceased loved one, then you may need to
choose a different appointment time. It could be that your angel
knows that this won't be an optimum time for your connection
(such as the angel foreseeing an unscheduled activity that would
interrupt you), or your deceased loved one may have a prior obli-
gation (such as performing service work, which most people do
in heaven).

Once you feel a sense of peace about your appointment time,
mentally tell the being about the physical location where you plan
to be. You are doing this for *your* sake, not for the heavenly being
(they can find you quite easily, no matter where you are). The point
is to have a clear mental image of your forthcoming appointment.
See yourself connecting with your angel, and hold a positive
expectation that you will have some breakthroughs with your angel
vision. Remember, your intentions create your experience. So, hold
an optimistic intention, without any sense of strain or urgency.

It's vital that you keep your appointment. If you truly can't
keep it or if you need to select a new location, then mentally
reschedule with your angel.

On the day of your appointment, arrive punctually with a pad
of paper and a medium-point pen. Sit down and mentally greet
your angel or deceased loved one. Close your eyes and breathe,
noticing the feeling that the being is with you. Mentally greet the
being, and begin having a mental conversation. Let the answers
come to you as feelings, words, thoughts, or visions.

Say a prayer for God's Divine light to surround you. Mentally
ask Archangel Michael to stay next to you during your appoint-

ment to ensure that only your angel or desired deceased loved one comes to you.

Then, open your eyes and write on the paper, "How can I see you?" Think the question as you write it. Write whatever impressions come to you, even if you seem to be receiving nothing. Automatic writing sometimes begins as a small trickle, but if you'll just write anything that pops into your mind, you'll start pulling the thread of the sweater. Keep going by writing other questions that you think of, and then write the impressions that come to you in response. Before long, you'll really be having conversations with heaven.

Your heavenly being will give you very helpful suggestions that will help you have angel visions. You may receive guidance to make lifestyle changes, meditate more often, or reframe your beliefs. By following your angels' step-by-step guidance, you'll be on your way to having angel visions. However, it is also very likely that you'll actually see your angel or deceased loved one during your appointment. Either way, keep going, and with practice and patience, you'll be having helpful and loving conversations with heaven on a regular basis.

Mirror work—For this exercise, you'll need a dimly lit room with a large mirror. You can do this exercise at night, using a night-light. But many people find it frightening to look in a mirror in the dark, so it's better to be in a diffused-light room during the day. So, cover your bathroom window with a thick towel, for instance.

Stand in front of the mirror and smile. When you do so, you'll automatically relax and make the exercise a more pleasant experience, instead of an intense or frightening one. You might even make funny faces in the mirror so that you'll laugh and relax even more. A secret to having angel visions is to be at ease and have fun during the entire process.

Then, with an "easy does it," nonchalant attitude, gaze into the mirror at yourself, and scan around your head and shoulders.

Don't try to force your angel vision; just allow anything that comes to you be a pleasant surprise. You may see a glowing aura around your head, and this vision may seem to be inside your mind. The whitish glow that you see is the aura of your guardian angels.

Focus on that whitish glow, and breathe in and out deeply. Mentally say to your angels, "I would like to see you now." You'll begin to see flashes of details of your angels. Keep looking above your shoulders. Don't focus directly on your own face, because it will seem to shift, and it may look like various other people during this exercise, which could greatly distract or even frighten you if you look at it. Your face is merely doing this because you are tapping into your own self's "Akashic Records," or the "Book of Life." You are seeing visions of your soul's recorded history.

So, having angel visions during this exercise is contingent upon keeping your gaze above your head and around your shoulders.

Dream work—You can mentally invite your deceased loved one, angel, or personal guide such as Jesus into your dreams at night. To have a powerful dreamtime angel vision, you'll need to have a virtually drug-free day. This means to avoid, or just take in a minimum of, caffeine, sugar, chocolate, alcohol, nicotine, chamomile, melatonin, valerian, and other mood- or energy-altering substances. These drugs and herbs inhibit your REM sleep cycle, thus reducing and altering your dream patterns.

Before you go to sleep at night, write on a piece of paper to whomever you are inviting into your dream: "I would like to talk with you and see you. I ask that you enter my dreams tonight. I love you and deeply desire to see you." Then, put this paper under your pillow, and mentally repeat this request as you're falling asleep.

As I mentioned in the Preface of this book, most dreamtime angel visions are extremely vivid. It is unlikely that you would forget a dream encounter with your angel or deceased loved one, especially if you go to sleep with a sober mind. However, it's always possible that your subconscious mind would cause you to forget having a dream if it knew that your waking mind couldn't handle this fact.

You may need to repeat this exercise for several days in a row before you actually have a dreamtime angel vision. And you may find that after you've asked for successive days to see your angel, your big dream occurs on the night when you just let it go and surrender the whole thing to God.

Looking sideways—After you meditate, mentally ask your angels or deceased loved one to appear to you. Then look out of the corner of your eye around the room. Some people have greater success seeing the spirit world out of the corner of their eye, rather than looking straight ahead. It seems that when we look out of the side of our eye, we're more open to seeing things that our forward vision may block out of conscious awareness.

Asking for a sign—Angel visions also include seeing "signs" in the physical world that are evidence of your angels' presence. You can mentally ask your angel or deceased loved one to send you a sign that will, for example, help you know which decision is best for you. You can also ask them to send you a sign just to let you know that they are with you.

You can specify exactly what type of sign you'd like to receive, or you can leave that up to your angels and deceased loved ones. Your task is to notice the sign as it is delivered. Fortunately, if you don't notice the sign at first, it will be repeated until you do. This repetition also helps allay any skepticism you may have about the validity of the sign.

Common signs include seeing feathers, birds, butterflies, rainbows, and flowers. You could also see license plates, billboards, or paintings that have significance to you. In addition, some signs are auditory, such as when you repeatedly hear a song that was meaningful to you and your deceased loved one, or when you hear ringing in one ear.

In addition, your angels may help you see glowing or sparkling lights, as a sign that they are near. These "angel trails" are the electrical spark of the heavenly beings moving across space.

No matter how clearly or how fuzzy your angel vision, it's essential to mentally thank God and the angels for their help. When we are happy, peaceful, and grateful, that is heaven's reward for all of the assistance that they give us.

)€)€)€

CHAPTER SIXTEEN

Everyday Angel Visions

A ngel visions aren't limited to seeing beings from heaven. Earth is populated with numerous angels, and you can easily see them with your physical eyes today. In this book, and also in my book *Healing with the Angels,* I've discussed angels who take human form. Sometimes these angels appear briefly during a crisis and then mysteriously disappear. Other times, the incarnated angels live a full human lifetime in a human body.

However, Earth angels take other forms. Part of our spiritual growth involves developing an awareness of the beauty and love that perpetually exists around us. As *A Course in Miracles* says, "I am blessed with gifts throughout the day." We just need to notice them.

Today, commit to noticing the angelic nature of people in your life, including your own self. Mentally note every time you see an act of love, no matter how subtle. If you see a child brush her sister's hair out of her eyes, or a pedestrian stop to pet a neighbor's dog, notice these angelic behaviors. If a co-worker spontaneously offers to jump in and help you with that last-minute report, mentally make a note of this gift from heaven.

The more we develop the habit of noticing "ordinary" miracles, the more apt we are to perceive the extraordinary ones. By training your mind and eyes to see only love, your whole body and being will start to attract more instances of love into your life.

You will draw in more guardian angels, since angelic beings (both Earthly and heavenly) are attracted to the light of loving people.

In other words, not all angel visions are mystical or other-worldly in nature. As an example:

An Earth Angel in My Life
by Anthony David Reid

It was my senior year of high school, and I had just finished playing in a basketball game. I had played a super game, which was fortunate, since I hated losing. In fact, I had expanded this hate for losing to hating my opponent. I hated everyone I played; I honestly believed that they were all bad people. Of course, I had never met any of them except on the playing field. I just hated them. Don't get me wrong—I wasn't a bad sportsman or a mean person. I was just extremely competitive.

As I left the gym, a young man stood in my path. He wasn't anyone I knew, so I started to walk by, but he reached out his hand to shake mine. I didn't take his right away, not knowing who he was. I looked at his face. I couldn't tell you exactly what he said to me, since that conversation took place 22 years ago. I *can* tell you that he congratulated me on a game well played. Okay, now I took his hand. He continued to congratulate me on the win and the great game. I was impressed by the fact that this praise would come from a complete stranger. He then left to allow me to go to the locker room.

When I entered the locker room, my coach was at the front door. He asked me what Jerry Koala and I were talking about. *That was Jerry Koala?* I asked. He nodded his head. Jerry Koala was the star of the other team. He hadn't played because of a sprained ankle. I learned for the first time that you can compete and be a class act at the same time. Jerry had the courage to acknowledge my performance, for the performance, not tarnished by who the performer was. This showed me that the opponents I was hating were not the bad people I had created in my mind. Jerry Koala was a good guy, and I liked him. My hate had no foundation; I had no reason to dislike my opponents outside the playing field. Two weeks later, with Jerry playing, his team beat mine 57–54 in the district tournament. His team won the next game and went on to the state tournament. For the first time, I was happy for an opponent.

A year later, I ran into Jerry in the cafeteria of the University of Northern Iowa. Neither one of us attended that school, but it just so happened that we both had girlfriends there. We talked for a couple of hours and became friends. Without realizing it, Jerry was the angel in my life who helped me find a path of brotherhood, one that accepted others' talents without jealousy. This lesson was a beginning of my understanding of the connection of all humanity. I am sure that God's angels had something to do with it.

Learning to Notice Angels Among You

I've noticed that people who have loving hearts are the very ones who usually have angel visions, positive mystical experiences, and wonderful synchronicities.

Part of the process of tuning into Earth angels is to lose our fear of other people. For instance, assure yourself that the vast majority of people that you'll meet would never purposely hurt you. In fact, total strangers would come immediately to your rescue if they noticed that you were hurt or suffering in any way. Just affirming that "everyone is a good person, just like me," helps us relax around other people. It also attunes our outlook so that we'll notice the good in ourselves . . . in others. And you probably know that your positive expectations will inspire other people to be their best when they're around you. Aren't you a nicer and happier person when you're with people who obviously like, respect, and honor you?

In heaven, everyone is cooperative and wears their happy heart on their sleeves. They don't pretend, or have their guard up, because there is nothing to defend against. The deceased people have taught me that we have similar opportunities on Earth. We can truly feel as if we're in heaven, surrounded by angels, if we look for the good in each person and situation.

As you drive down the street, allow yourself to feel gratitude in your heart for all the people you see. Know that they are on your side and that they would truly act like guardian angels for you if an emergency occurred near them. And for all we know, one or two of the people whom you see on your way to work—or even *at* work—could be angels in disguise.

Today, make it your intention to notice the angelic actions that people engage in. Notice when a stranger helps another, when someone smiles at another individual, or when a person gives directions to other drivers or allows them to merge in ahead of their car. Notice your own angelic actions toward strangers.

By training your mind and heart to notice the many Earthly angels around you, your heart will open up to the angels who live in heaven's dimension. A grateful heart is an unafraid heart, and the more that you can rid yourself of fear, the more likely it is that you will soon be able to see angels of all types around you.

Happy angel visions!

〉€ 〉€ 〉€

Bibliography

Preface

1. MacDonald, William L. (1995). The effects of religiosity and structural strain on reported paranormal experiences. *Journal for the Scientific Study of Religion*, Vol. 34, pp. 366–376.

2. Gill Fry interviewed Emma Heathcote for Share International Media Service (1999). Data used with permission of Emma Heathcote.

3. Stevenson, I., 1982. "The Contribution of Apparitions to the Evidence for Survival." *The Journal of the American Society for Psychical Research,* Vol. 76, pp. 341–358.

4. Stevenson, I., op. cit.

5. Greeley, A.M. and Hout, M., 1998. "Pie in the Sky While You're Alive: Americans' Belief in Life After Death and Supply-Side Religion."

6. Stevenson, I., Ibid.

7. Palmer, J., 1979. "A Community Mail Survey of Psychic Experiences." *Journal of the American Society of Psychical Research,* Vol. 73, pp. 221–251.

8. Stevenson, I., 1992. "A Series of Possibly Paranormal Recurrent Dreams." *Journal of Scientific Exploration,* Vol. 6, No. 3, pp. 281–289.

9. Stevenson, I., 1983. "Do We Need a New Word to Supplement 'Hallucination'?" *American Journal of Psychiatry,* Vol. 140, No. 12, pp. 1609–1611.

West, D.J., 1960. "Visionary and Hallucinatory Experiences: A Comparative Appraisal." *International Journal of Parapsychology,* Vol. 2, No. 1, pp. 89–100.

10. Osis, K. and Erlendur, H., 1997. *At the Hour of Death.* Third Edition (Norwalk, CT: Hastings House).

11. *The Bible.* Hebrews 13:2.

Chapter Thirteen
1. *The Bible*, 1 Corinthians 13 and 14.

Chapter Fourteen
1. Isis, K. and Erlendur, H., 1997. *At the Hour of Death.* Third Edition (Norwalk, CT: Hastings House).

❧ ❧ ❧

About the Author

Doreen Virtue, Ph.D., is a spiritual doctor of psychology who works with the angelic realm. A clairvoyant since childhood, Doreen teaches people practical ways to work with heaven to heal their lives. She is the author of many works, including *Healing with the Angels, Angel Therapy, Divine Guidance,* the audio program *Connecting with Your Angels,* and *Healing with the Angels Oracle Cards.*

Dr. Virtue gives angel readings at workshops across North America each weekend; and she teaches audience members how to see, hear, feel, and know their guardian angels. She has appeared on *Oprah,* CNN, *The View,* and other talk shows, where she is frequently referred to as "The Angel Lady."

Dr. Virtue welcomes your angel stories for her books, and you can submit them to her at **AngelStories@AngelTherapy.com,** or by regular mail in care of Hay House. Please be sure to indicate your permission to publish your story, and let her know if you want the story published anonymously or with your real name. For information on Dr. Virtue's workshops, please visit her Website at: **AngelTherapy.com.**

Other Hay House Titles of Related Interest

Books

Adventures of a Psychic: *The Fascinating and Inspiring True-Life Story of One of America's Most Successful Clairvoyants,* by Sylvia Browne

The Alchemist's Handbook, by John Randolph Price

Born to Be Together: *Love Relationships, Astrology, and the Soul,* by Terry Lamb

The Experience of God: *How 40 Well-Known Seekers Encounter the Sacred,* by Jonathan Robinson

God, Creation, and Tools for Life, by Sylvia Browne

The Indigo Children: *The New Kids Have Arrived,* by Lee Carroll and Jan Tober

Audio Programs

Angels and Spirit Guides: *How to Call Upon Your Angels and Spirit Guide for Help,* by Sylvia Browne

Developing Your Own Psychic Powers, by John Edward

Journeys into Past Lives, by Denise Linn

Making Contact with the Other Side, by Sylvia Browne